A Guide for

英汉对照

第二版

英语导游服务能力

问与答

主　编◎朱　宁
参　编◎王伟民
吴本南
刘　斌

北京·旅游教育出版社

图书在版编目（CIP）数据
英语导游服务能力问与答 / 朱宁主编. -- 2版.
北京 : 旅游教育出版社, 2025. 3. -- ISBN 978-7-5637-4861-7
Ⅰ. F590.63-44
中国国家版本馆CIP数据核字第2025S5A733号

A Guide for Tour Guides
英语导游服务能力问与答
（第二版）
主编　朱宁
参编　王伟民　吴本南　刘斌

策　　划	李红丽
责任编辑	李红丽
出版单位	旅游教育出版社
地　　址	北京市朝阳区定福庄南里 1 号
邮　　编	100024
发行电话	（010）65778403　65728372　65767462（传真）
本社网址	www.tepcb.com
E - mail	tepfx@163.com
排版单位	北京旅教文化传播有限公司
印刷单位	天津雅泽印刷有限公司
经销单位	新华书店
开　　本	787毫米×1092毫米　1/32
印　　张	8
字　　数	135 千字
版　　次	2025 年 3 月第 2 版
印　　次	2025 年 3 月第 1 次印刷
定　　价	39.80 元

（图书如有装订差错请与发行部联系）

再版前言

REVISED PREFACE

本书前身为2016年出版的《导游服务能力100问》（英汉对照）。2018年，为提升书籍的针对性和实用性，我们广泛听取国内外资深导游与领队的建议，并深入研究各省市导游资格考试“科目五 导游服务能力”大纲，提炼考点、优化表述，对原书进行了修订。为更清晰地定位主要读者群——英语导游，修订版更名为《英语导游服务能力问与答》。

近年来，导游服务面临的市场需求、政策背景、法治环境、管理要求等均发生了较大的变化。2023年以来，我国相继出台多项优化入境旅游发展的措施，推动了入境旅游市场的繁荣。2024年，为适应消费升级和行业发展需要，促进导游服务水平提升，推动旅游业高质量发展，文化和旅游部发布了新版《导游服务规范》国家标准。在这样的背景下，本书进行了新一轮的修订。

本书涵盖了导游资格考试科目五中“语言和礼貌礼仪”“导游服务规范”及“应变能力”等多项全国通用板块的内容。此外，针对近年来部分省市考试大纲对领队服务要求的增加和强化，本书特别补充了领队相关工作要点。

本书共分为五个部分，包括“地陪服务流程与规范”“领队和全陪服务流程与规范”“特殊旅游群体服务”“导游应变能力”和“导游带团艺术”。全书总结了178个导游服务规范及服务过程中的常见问题，采用一问一答、英汉对照的形式呈现，用简洁凝练的语言明确操作步骤与应对建议，力求针对性与实用性兼备。此外，本书所有英文内容均配有 MP3 音频，以二维码链接的形式呈现，扫码即可收听。

本书由上海旅游高等专科学校副教授、高级英语导游朱宁主笔，特级英语导游王伟民老师、上海导游培训资深专家吴本南老师，以及上海旅游高等专科学校刘斌副教授参与编写。

在本书编写过程中，应国宏老师、张尚华老师、朱晓霞老师、赵佩章老师等行业专家提出了许多有价值的建议；上海旅游高等专科学校王缇萦老师和吴云老师给予了大力支持；同校的赵宝国老师作为笔者导游之路的引路人，自始至终给予关心和指导，在此特向他们表示衷心的感谢。另外，在编写过程中，我们还参考了相关书籍，在此也对参考资料的作者们一并表示感谢。

希望本书可以为参加导游资格考试的考生提供有价值的参考，并期待它成为新手导游朋友“实用、好用、够用”的工作指导手册。

朱　宁

于上海旅游高等专科学校

目 录
CONTENTS

Part Ⅰ The Local Guide 地陪服务流程与规范

Part Ⅱ The Tour Leader and the National Guide 领队和全陪服务流程与规范

Part Ⅲ Special Care for Special Groups 特殊旅游群体服务

Part V The Art of Managing a Tour
导游带团艺术

Part Ⅰ The Local Guide

地陪服务流程与规范

听力音频

Unit 1 Basic Requirements for Tour Guides 导游服务基本规范

001. What are the basic guidelines for a tour guide?（导游服务的基本原则是什么？）

★ Fulfill the tourism agreement or contract.

★ Combine quality service with special care to special cases.

★ Protect the legitimate rights and interests of tourists.

★ Maintain the good image, reputation and interests of the company the tour guide works for.

☆ 严格按照旅游合同办事。

☆ 服务至诚，遵循优质服务和特殊情况特殊处理的原则。

☆ 以游客为本，维护游客合法权益。

☆ 维护公司的良好形象、声誉和利益。

002. What are the proper manners for a tour guide?（导游服务时应遵循什么样的行为规范？）

★ Be Law-abiding and provide different information for different groups (Keep some information from inbound groups).

★ Strictly follow the reporting-and-instructing system.

★ Wear tour guide license when providing services.

★ Have a warm smile and a friendly attitude; treat tourists with the same care and concern that would be extended to your own family members; when tourists have problems, put yourself in their shoes.

★ Maintain a good personal image.

☆ 遵纪守法，提供服务时注意内外有别。

☆ 严格遵守请示报告制度。

☆ 从事业务活动时佩戴导游证。

☆ 微笑服务，礼貌待客；对旅游者一视同仁，提供周到服务；旅游者遇到困难时，能换位思考，提供帮助。

☆ 保持良好的个人形象。

【备注】“旅游者”一词英文可用 guests, travelers, tourists, clients 等，《旅游法》中采用 tourists 一词，故文中凡涉及旅游者，英文均用 tourists。《旅游法》中“导游”一词英文采用 the tour guide，本书采用相同表述且如无特别标注，本书中 the tour guide 均指地陪。工作中，不少导游习惯用“办公室”（office）一词指代“旅行社”，本书沿用此做法，英文用 office 指代 travel agency。

003. What is considered the proper dress for a tour guide?（导游应如何着装？）

★ Professional attire is appropriate for the first day to meet the group.

★ When conducting tours, smart casual and business casual are fine.

★ Female tour guides — No heavy make-up, short skirts or hot pants.

★ Male tour guides — No short pants and no shirts with logos of other travel companies; socks are required.

★ Unacceptable for either gender: loud clothes, ripped clothing, clothing which has or is in the process of being rumpled, T-shirts, underwear as outerwear, flip-flops and inappropriately revealing attire such as a bare midriff.

★ Caps are not to be worn backwards, sideways or tilted.

☆ 接团首日以职业装为宜。

☆ 带团中，应穿着大方、休闲得体。

☆ 女性导游不化浓妆，不穿短裙、热裤。

☆ 男性导游不穿短裤，不穿印有其他旅行社标识的广告，不光脚穿鞋。

☆ 导游不穿过于花哨的衣服、不穿人为做破做皱的衣服（如被当成时髦的破洞牛仔裤等），不穿T恤衫，不可内衣外穿，不穿夹脚拖鞋，不穿暴露的衣服（如露脐装）。

☆ 不反戴帽子、不歪戴帽子。

【备注】得体的着装是导游服务的重要组成部分。有经验的导游会根据旅游者的特点选择着装。Smart Casual 的穿着一定要"简约"，但不能"简便"；要"随意"，但不能"随便"，虽一字之差却有很大差别；裤装或裙装可以穿得比较休闲，但不可以非常贴身；颜色纯粹不花哨，比如海军蓝、黑色、灰色、棕色、米色之类都是日常之选，肯定不会出错；裙子长度则至少要及膝，坐下时足以遮住大腿；长裙若是开衩，衩口不应该高过膝盖；上衣除衬衣之外，修身的针织衫同样属于 Smart Casual 的范畴。"loud clothes"指"花哨的衣服"。

004. How can a tour guide make a good first impression on tourists?（导游如何给旅游者留下良好的第一印象？）

★ Have a good personal hygiene. (Make sure you shower, shave and brush/comb your hair; pay particular attention to your oral hygiene.)

★ Keep good image. (Dress in business casual attire and wear comfortable shoes; make sure all your clothing is clean, pressed and in good condition; female guides may wear a modest amount of make-up; bring a small bag/backpack to carry your paper work, city maps for tourists, pen/marker and note-paper, personal electronics, batteries/chargers, a medical first-aid kit, water, small snacks, personal items, etc.)

★ Suitable attitude and behavior are required (which may suggest good professional quality and help win trust and support of tourists).

★ Pay attention to pronunciation and intonation; make a

good welcome speech and address it clearly with simple sentences.

☆ 搞好个人卫生（洗澡、修面、梳头，尤其要注意口腔卫生）。
☆ 保持良好的仪容仪表（着装以商务休闲服和舒服的鞋子为宜；衣服干净、熨烫得体；女性导游可化淡妆；将纸质材料、地图、笔、便签、电子产品、电池、充电器、药品包、水、小零食、地图及其他个人物品放入随身携带的背包）。
☆ 保持得体的仪态和行为（这会在某种程度上体现导游的职业素养，从而有助于导游赢得旅游者的信任与支持）。
☆ 注意语音语调；用简洁明了的语言致欢迎词。

【备注】体态得当通常包括坐姿、站姿和手势。前倾 12 度的坐姿，挺胸收腹，略收下颌，保持与客人目光平视的站姿，掌心向上的手势都可以展示良好的个人工作仪态。

005. What are the key requirements for tour guide service competency?（导游服务能力要求包括哪些？）

★ Professional ethics.
★ Professional skills and personal competency (including language proficiency, hospitality and operational

abilities, and IT application skills).

★ Industry knowledge.

★ Professional demeanor.

☆ 思想素质。

☆ 技术技能（包括语言能力、接待操作能力和信息技术应用能力）。

☆ 业务知识。

☆ 职业形象。

006. What are the requirements for good language competence of a tour guide?（良好的导游语言表达能力包括哪些？）

★ Let yourself be heard. (If you need a loudspeaker, check it in advance.)

★ Good pronunciation, moderate speed, proper punctuation and appropriate body language.

★ Express yourself clearly with enthusiasm and make yourself be fully understood. (Speak to the point instead of beating around the bush; use plain and simple language; avoid using too many discourse markers and pet phrases; Do not switch from different languages.)

☆ 确保旅游者能听清导游的声音。（如果需要使用扩音设备，要事先做好检查。）

☆ 发音准确、语速适宜、停顿得当，合理使用体态语言。

☆ 正确、清楚、生动、灵活地讲解交流。（直指要点，避免顾左右而言他；选择通俗易懂、好记忆的语言表述；尽量克服多余的语气词、口头禅、双语症。）

【备注】外语导游的语言能力在接待中起着举足轻重的作用。接待外国旅游者时，尤其要谨慎使用“我发誓”“我保证”等表述。在有效沟通中，始终保持友好、礼貌和尊重的态度；此外，怎么说比说什么更重要，讲解交流中要特别注意方式方法。

007. What are the eight working procedures of the local guide services?（地陪服务的八大工作流程包括哪些？）

★ Preparation.

★ Meeting the group.

★ Hotel check-in.

★ Checking the itinerary with the tour leader/national guide.

★ Sightseeing.

★ Other services (catering, shopping and entertainment, etc.).

★ Hotel check-out and departure.

★ Follow-up work.

☆ 接待准备工作。

☆ 迎接服务。

☆ 入住酒店服务。
☆ 与领队（全陪）核实商定日程。
☆ 参观游览服务。
☆ 其他服务（如餐饮、购物和娱乐等）。
☆ 酒店退房及送客服务。
☆ 后续工作。

Related words and phrases

organizing travel agency/travel company	组团社
local travel agency/tour operator	地接社
working relationship	工作关系
tourist-generating country/source country	客源国
tourist agreement	旅游协议/合同
package tourism contract	包价旅游合同
name tag	导游胸卡
tour banner/tour guide banner	旅行社徽旗/导游旗
tour guide	导游
national guide	全陪导游/全陪
local tour guide	地陪导游/地陪
tour lead/tour escort/tour leader	领队

【备注】组团社是指与旅游者订立包价旅游合同的旅行社。地接社指接受组团社委托，在目的地接待旅游者的旅行社。“组团社”一词英文可用 travel company 或 organizing travel agency，《旅游法》中采用的是 organizing travel agency，“地

接社”一词英文可用 local travel agency 或 tour operator，《旅游法》采用的是 local travel agency。书中涉及以上所指，均采用《旅游法》中的表述。包价旅游合同，是指旅行社预先安排行程，提供或者通过履行辅助人提供交通、住宿、餐饮、游览、导游或者领队等两项以上旅游服务，旅游者以总价支付旅游费用的合同。

Questions for discussion

1. Why is it important for a tour guide to have the ability to apply information technology?
2. What kind of professional skills should a tour guide have?
3. What kind of industry knowledge or professional knowledge should a tour guide have?

听力音频

Unit 2 Preparation and Meeting a Group
准备与接站服务

008. What kind of preparation should a tour guide make before meeting a group?（接团前，导游应做好哪些准备工作？）

★ Necessary items: keep in hand all the necessary items such as the guiding license, the group itinerary, the tour guide banner and the evaluation form.

★ Image preparation: try to leave a good first impression on the group.

★ Psychological preparation: be confident, hardworking and get yourself prepared for difficulties.

★ Knowledge preparation: be familiar with all the programs included in the itinerary and be capable of giving relevant presentation.

★ Itinerary preparation: be familiar with itinerary details including meals/restaurants, scenic spots, special arrangements and special requests, if any.

☆ 物质准备：随身携带导游证、行程单、导游旗及反馈表等。

☆ 形象准备：争取留下良好的第一印象。

☆ 心理准备：自信、勤奋，做好面对各种困难的准备。

☆ 知识准备：熟悉行程中所有景点并能做出相关讲解。

☆ 计划准备：了解包括餐饮安排、游览景点、有无特殊要求等行程细节。

【备注】除以上准备外，导游还应提前与相关接待单位或个人联络沟通，以确保旅游接待的诸多事宜得到妥善安排。联络沟通内容主要包括：落实旅游者的交通、食宿、票务、活动等事宜；确认旅游者所乘交通工具及其确切抵达时间；与旅游客车司机联系，确定会面时间和车辆停放位置。

009. What items should a tour guide prepare before meeting a group?（接团前，导游应做什么物品准备？）

★ Paper work: itineraries, evaluation forms, ticket settlement sheets, settlement sheets for the national guide.

★ Professional items: loudspeakers, tour guide banners, tour guide certificates, business cards, city maps, pens and notebooks.

★ Personal items: necessary medicine, water, small snacks, personal electronics such as phones, batteries, chargers, power bank, etc.

☆ 计划单据：接待计划、质量反馈表、门票结算单、全陪结算单。

☆ 工作物件：扩音器、导游旗（检查旗面）、导游证、名片、地图、笔、便签等。

☆ 个人物品：通常包括自备药品、水、小食品及个人电子产品，如手机、电池、充电器、充电宝等。

010. What kind of psychological preparation should a tour guide go through before starting a tour? （接团前，导游应有怎样的心理准备？）

Psychological preparation is important for tour guides. Only if they are well prepared in the following aspects, can they solve various problems.

★ Firstly, be confident. (Though tourists are from different countries, having different background, they are strangers in a new city. The tour guide can always show them something new, something special in his/her city.)

★ Secondly, the tour guide should know that being a tour guide means he/she should be hardworking all the time. (He/She should improve himself/herself in many aspects because a qualified tour guide is expected to know something of everything and everything of something as well.)

★ Thirdly, be prepared for various difficulties. (The tour guide should understand that even he/she has tried his/her best to offer the best service for tourists, sometimes he/she will have to face various complaints. And in such a case, the tour guide should be calm and try to find ways to solve the problem and improve his/ her service.)

对导游来说，做好充分的心理准备很重要。只有准备充分，才可能解决有可能出现的各种状况。

☆ 首先，导游必须自信。（虽然旅游者来自不同国家，背景各异，但他们是导游所在城市的客人。导游总能展示一些新的、独特的城市风情给旅游者。）

☆ 其次，导游应当明了从事这一职业意味着要始终努力。（导游应当在各方面提升自己，因为一名合格的导游既要有广泛的知识，也要对某一领域较为精通。）

☆ 最后，导游应做好面对各种困难的准备。（导游应当清楚即便他/她竭尽全力提供优质服务，难免还是会遇到投诉。在这种情况下，导游应当保持冷静，解决问题并提升服务质量。）

011. What kind of knowledge preparation should a tour guide make?（接团前，导游应做什么知识准备？）

★ Be familiar with the tourist generating countries and other relevant knowledge.

★ Be well prepared for translating vocabularies in certain fields if there are any.

★ If the tour guide is not familiar with the attractions, he/

she should either visit the attractions in advance or collect necessary information.

★ Be well prepared for some hot topics and latest news in which tourists may be interested.

☆ 根据旅游团的情况做客源国及专业知识准备。
☆ 做好翻译准备，如相关领域的词汇翻译。
☆ 不熟悉的景点要踩点和查阅资料。
☆ 准备国内外新闻和旅游者可能感兴趣的话题。

012. What should a tour guide be familiar with when he is making itinerary preparation?（导游在熟悉接待计划时要注意哪些方面？）

★ Information concerning the group (the name of the travel company, name and code of the group, name and telephone number of the contact person; generating country, number of group members, language; names and phone numbers of the tour leader and national guide, way of settlement, complete itinerary of the group, cities of entry and exit).

★ Information concerning tourists (names, occupations, genders, ages, religions, special requirements, the tour leader, central characters in the group).

★ Arrangements specified in the itinerary (arrival and departure arrangement, food and beverage, accommodation, traffic tickets, attractions, entertainment and shopping).

☆ 旅游团基本情况（海内外组团社名称、旅游团名称团号、联系人姓名电话；国别、人数、语言；领队全陪姓名电话、结算方式、全程路线和出入境地点）。
☆ 旅游团成员情况（姓名、职业、性别、年龄、宗教、特殊要求，领队情况及个别重点人物的情况）。
☆ 旅游团行程安排（抵离、餐饮、住宿、交通票、游览景点、娱乐及购物安排）。

013. As a tour guide, what are you supposed to do before meeting a group at the airport?（去机场接机前，导游应做哪些准备？）

★ Confirm details of the arrival time, the port of entry/exit, transportation means, hotel accommodation and arrangement of luggage delivery.
★ Make sure you will get to the airport at least 30 minutes before the plane lands.
★ Make sure the coach is clean and in excellent working order, and will arrive on time. Confirm with the driver where the coach will be for boarding.
★ Get familiar with the basic information of tourists (including the number of tourists and their nationality, gender, occupation, age, religion and special requests).
★ Know some important information of the group

(including the name of the organizing travel agency, group code, the liaison person in charge of the group, the name of the tour leader/national guide and his/her cell phone number).

☆ 确认航班抵达准确时间、出入境口岸、交通、住宿安排、行李接送等。
☆ 至少提前 30 分钟抵达机场。
☆ 确保旅游车准时到位，车况良好，与司机确认上车地点。
☆ 再次熟悉旅行团成员基本信息(包括团员人数、国籍、性别、职业、年龄、宗教信仰以及特殊要求等）。
☆ 再次熟悉旅行团重要信息（包括组团社名称、团号、组团社联系人、领队/全陪姓名及手机号）。

【备注】在确认车况环节，尤其要注意车载话筒是否有问题。在实际操作中，因客人出关有很多手续要办理，一般需要 1 小时左右，所以不少有经验的导游会掐好时间抵达机场。另外，航班晚点时有发生，为避免长时间等候，接机前应确认航班抵达具体信息。多年来，因各种延误原因，航班正常率饱受诟病。据民航局 2020 年发布的《2019 年民航行业发展统计公报》显示，全国客运航空公司平均航班正常率为 81.65%，航班平均延误时间为 14 分钟。

014. What are you supposed to do at the arrival gate of the airport?（在机场接机时，导游应如何操作？）

★ Hold, at least above the shoulder, the welcome sign of the organizing travel agency or that of the local travel agency at the arrival gate to make sure that tourists can easily identify you.

★ Confirm some important information and make sure you are receiving the right group.

★ Greet the group and arrange luggage delivery.

★ Briefly talk with the tour lead to know something more about the group.

★ Lead the tourists to the parking lot.

☆ 在抵达出口醒目位置高举写有组团社或地接社名字的欢迎牌（至少要高于肩部），使旅游者能及时看到。

☆ 核对信息，确定没有接错团。

☆ 欢迎旅游团，安排行李接送。

☆ 向领队询问团队情况。

☆ 带领旅游者去停车场。

015. How can you avoid picking up a wrong group?（导游如何避免接错团？）

★ Make sure you are in the right airport and be there 30 minutes earlier than the arrival time.

★ Be familiar with the basic group information.

★ Stand in plain sight with the welcome sign and make sure that all groups will see you before they pass by.

★ Look for those whose characteristics are in accordance with your target group.

★ Carefully confirm the name and the cell phone number of the tour leader when the target group shows up.

☆ 提前 30 分钟到达机场，确认没有去错机场。

☆ 熟悉旅行团基本信息。

☆ 高举欢迎牌，站在醒目的地方，尽量确保每个团队经过时都能看到。（被动——对方辨认）

☆ 寻找与目标团队特点相符的人群。（主动——己方辨认）

☆ 当特征符合的旅行团出现时，主动上前询问，认真核对领队姓名及电话号码。

016. How can you avoid missing a group at the airport or the railway station?（导游如何预防漏接事故？）

★ Read the itinerary carefully.

★ Confirm the exact arrival time and make sure you are in the right airport or railway station.

★ Get to the airport or the railway station 30 minutes before the arrival time.

☆ 认真仔细地阅读接待计划。

☆ 核实交通工具抵达的准确时间和地点。

☆ 提前半小时到达接站地点。

【备注】不少城市有两个机场、多个火车站，有时接送客人的机场、火车站不同，导游需要特别注意接送站的具体地址。有些团队的抵达时间因种种原因会有变化，对此类情况，导游需要特别注意，细心核实。

017. How will you handle the luggage at the port of entry?（导游应如何处理入境团队的行李？）

★ If there is a luggage handler from the local travel agency, place the luggage in the designated area for transfer.

★ Count the number of pieces with the tour leader and the luggage handler.

★ Tie a luggage tag onto one piece of luggage with the exact number written on it before leaving them to the luggage handler.

★ If the luggage goes with the coach, make sure the tourists see all of their own bags before loading.

☆ 如地接社安排了行李员，让旅游者把行李放置在指定地点。

☆ 与领队和行李员共同确认行李件数。

☆ 与行李员交接时，将写有确切行李件数的地接社行李标签系于行李上。

☆ 如行李随车携带，确保每位旅游者上车前看到自己的行李，然后再装车。

【备注】处理团队行李，基本有两种情况。一是安排行李员处理，二是行李随车。回答问题时，应分清情况，分别作答。

018. What kind of services should be provided when tourists are on boarding?（在引导旅游者登车的过程中，导游应提供怎样的服务？）

★ Hold the tour guide banner, leading tourists to the coach.
★ Help the driver place large pieces of luggage.
★ Stand by the door, helping those who need your help.
★ Check the luggage rack.
★ Politely count the number of tourists.

☆ 持导游旗、引导登车。
☆ 帮助司机安放大件行李。
☆ 站车门一侧，如客人需要帮助，协助登车。
☆ 检查行李架。
☆ 礼貌清点人数。

019. What is the counting technique on the coach?（导游如何在旅游客车上清点人数？）

★ Count the number of tourists politely and efficiently.

★ Count in mind and do not count with your fingers.

★ Count the vacant/empty seats if the coach is nearly full.

☆ 礼貌而高效地清点人数。

☆ 心中默数，勿用手指清点。

☆ 如旅游客车几乎满员，可清点空座位(也可根据情况，用分组、点名等方式)。

Related words and phrases

domestic/international flight	国内/国际航班
terminal	航站楼/终点站
regular/extra flight	定期航班/加班航班
charter	包机
non-stop (direct flight can have a stop)	直达航班
red-eye flight	红眼航班
luggage/baggage	行李
carry-on luggage	手提行李
checked luggage	托运行李
luggage/bag claim	行李提取
luggage carousel	行李传送带
luggage claim office	行李认领处
immigration control/emigration control	入境/出境检查
customs formalities	海关手续
customs declaration form	报关单
port of entry/exit	入境口岸/出境口岸

【备注】luggage 和 baggage 均表示行李，英国人较多用 luggage，美国人多用 baggage。

Questions for discussion

1. You are suddenly sent to meet a group at the airport and informed that the driver with the coach is already there. What will you do when you get there?
2. You are at the Pudong International Airport, expecting a group from Singapore. How can you identify your group as quickly as possible at the arrival gate?
3. A group from the United States has just arrived at Pudong International Airport. What will you do when the tour leader tells you that a piece of luggage is missing?

听力音频

Unit 3 On the Way to Hotel and Helping Check-in

去酒店途中及协助办理入住

020. What are you supposed to tell your group on the way from the airport to the hotel?（在从机场去酒店的途中，导游应向旅游者提供哪些信息？）

★ Present a welcome speech to the group.

★ Give a simple picture of your city (history, geography, population, size and climate, etc).

★ If the group is from overseas and makes your city the first stop, make sure their watches show the local time.

★ If possible, present city maps to tourists and show them where they are and where they will be. (If maps are not available on the coach, get them in the hotel.)

★ Go through the schedule briefly.

★ Tell them Dos and Don'ts in your country (water drinkable or not, currencies and where to change).

★ Show the tourists impressive structures, beautiful scenes and places of interest on both sides of the road.

★ Shortly before arriving at the hotel, provide basic information about the hotel facilities.

☆ 致欢迎词。

☆ 简要介绍城市概况（如历史、地理、人口、面积、气候等）。

☆ 如旅游者来自海外，而导游所在城市为该旅行团入境第一站，提醒旅游者把表调整至当地时间。

☆ 向旅游者发放地图，指明旅游团目前所在位置及将要到达的地方（如车上未备地图，可在酒店索取）。

☆ 简要介绍旅游行程。

☆ 注意事项介绍（如自来水是否可以直接喝、何处兑换货币等）。

☆ 沿途风光或主要景观介绍。

☆ 到达宾馆前，简要介绍宾馆设施。

【备注】导游可在下车前说明并提醒：宾馆房间的部分食品和物品为有偿消费，配有卡片标注消费价格，请旅游者明白消费；另外，提醒海外旅游者，在中国自来水不能直接饮用。

021. What should be included in a welcome speech?
（欢迎词应包括哪些部分？）

★ Welcome tourists.

★ Introduce yourself and the driver to the whole group.

★ Briefly introduce the schedule.

★ Tell them your group will provide good service to them.

★ Ask if they have any questions.

★ Express your sincere hope that they have a wonderful trip in your city.

☆ 表达欢迎之意。

☆ 向旅游者介绍自己和司机。

☆ 旅游日程简介。

☆ 表达提供优质服务的愿望。

☆ 询问旅游者是否有问题。

☆ 祝愿旅游者在逗留期间旅途愉快。

【备注】欢迎词中旅游日程简介仅仅是提及，不可展开细说。

022. Make a brief welcome speech.（致一个简短的欢迎词。）

★ Good morning, ladies and gentlemen. Welcome to Shanghai. On behalf of ABC Travel Agency, I'd like to extend our warm welcome to all of you. My name is Mary and I will be your local guide for the next several days. Mr. Wang is our driver. He is a very experienced driver and he has worked for the company for 15 years. My telephone number is 186-1234-5678. And the number of the coach is 98765. In the following days, we will visit some popular scenic spots in Shanghai and also we will go to Suzhou for its classical gardens. I believe you will soon love this city as I do. We will try our best to make your trip here a pleasant one. If you have any questions, please don't hesitate to ask me and I shall be very pleased to answer. Hope you enjoy your stay in Shanghai.

☆ 女士们，先生们，早上好。欢迎来到上海。我代表ABC旅行社向大家表示热烈的欢迎。我叫玛丽，是接下来几天的导游。王先生是我们的司机。他是一位很有经验的司机，已经为公司工作了15年。我的电话号码是18612345678。本车车牌号是98765。

☆ 在接下来的几天里，我们将游览上海的一些热门景点，也将去苏州参观古典园林。我相信大家很快会和我一样喜欢上这个城市。

☆ 我们将尽最大的努力使您的旅途愉快。如果您有任何问题，请随时问我，我很高兴为您解答。

☆ 希望大家在上海玩得愉快。

【备注】以上是一篇最简单的欢迎词，以涵盖欢迎词各组成部分为标准。在实际工作中，一篇优秀的欢迎词可以帮助导游给旅游者留下良好的第一印象，因而导游要精心准备既涵盖基本要点又富有个人特点的欢迎词。此外，越来越多的导游在欢迎词中会介绍自己的中文名字，并解释其中的含义，并教会外国旅游者简单的发音，这也不失为一种传播中国文化的方式。

023. What help can you offer when the group is doing the check-in at the hotel?（地陪应如何协助旅游团办理入住手续？）

★ Assist the tour leader to collect passports (to be scanned) and return them to tourists as soon as possible.

★ Point out hotel facilities to tourists (including the

location of the cashier, dining room for breakfast and business center).

★ Get hotel business cards and give one to each tourist.

★ Assist the tour leader to distribute room keys.

★ Arrange luggage delivery to tourists' rooms.

★ After the tourists go to their rooms, wait in the lobby for another 15 minutes in case they need your further assistance.

★ Ask the front desk for an up-to-date rooming list for your own reference.

☆ 协助领队收集护照(以便扫描)并及时归还给旅游者。

☆ 介绍宾馆设施分布(包括外币兑换处、早餐用餐地点及商务中心等)。

☆ 协助领队分发房卡。

☆ 安排行李进房。

☆ 旅游者入住后在大堂等候 15 分钟左右,以处理可能出现的问题。

☆ 向前台要一份旅游者的最新住房表以备用。

【备注】如需安排叫早,最好在车上跟旅游者确认好时间,以免在宾馆大堂旅游者没有听清。安排叫早时,确认使用的是最终的旅游者住房表。如此前没有将手机号留给领队,在入住办理完成后,将号码留给领队。

Related words and phrases

rooming list	分房名单
single room	单人间
twin(-bed) room	双床间（两张单人床）
double room	大床间/双人间（一张双人床）
triple room	三人间
standard room	标间
suite	套房
deluxe room	豪华间
room with king-size bed	大床间
presidential suite	总统套房
check-in service	入住登记服务
check out	退房
registration form	住宿登记表
room service	客房送餐服务
hotel lobby	宾馆大堂

Questions for discussion

1. What would you do when some tourists want to move from a 3-star hotel to a 4-star hotel?
2. If a tourist refuses to share a twin room with his/her roommate and asks for a single room, what should the local guide do?

听力音频

Unit 4 At the Restaurant 用餐服务

024. What are you supposed to do before going to the restaurant?（去餐厅用餐前，导游应做哪些核对工作？）

★ Call and confirm the time, the number of the tourists, place for meals, the rate and beverage policy of the group meal.

★ Make sure the special arrangements already mentioned in the contract are followed.

★ Tell the restaurant any new requests raised by tourists due to various reasons.

☆ 电话确认用餐时间、用餐人数及地点，确认用餐标准和酒水标准。

☆ 确认在合同中明确的个别特殊用餐安排。

☆ 将个别旅游者因特殊原因而提出的用餐要求告知餐厅。

【备注】餐饮服务中最常见的是清真、素食和过敏这三大特殊用餐要求。三大特殊用餐要求必须慎重对待，细心落实。提前电话核实用餐安排，在旺季可以更有效地减少等待时间。

025. What kind of services can you offer during the meal?（旅游者用餐时，导游应提供什么服务？）

★ Help with seating the tourists.
★ Let the staff know who needs what service.
★ Make sure the food is fresh with appropriate temperature and up to the standards specified in the contract.
★ Inform the tourists of the ingredients of some dishes and point out spicy dishes.
★ Share the culture behind the dishes with local flavor.
★ Answer questions if there are any.

☆ 协助旅游者入座。
☆ 告诉服务员哪些旅游者需要特别的餐饮服务。
☆ 确保餐厅提供热的和新鲜的食物，并达到合同规定的标准。
☆ 介绍菜肴的成分，指出辛辣菜肴（有的旅游者不能吃辣的食物）。
☆ 向旅游者介绍本地菜肴的特点和与之有关的文化。
☆ 解答旅游者的问题。

【备注】欧美旅游者在吃中餐时，习惯先将菜肴放入自己盘中再吃，因此上菜时要确保每桌有餐巾纸一叠，每道菜配有一把公勺。如条件许可，为有需求的旅游者同时提供筷子和刀叉。如有旅游者提出增加就餐标准之外的饮料，通常要告知旅游者需要现金现付。用餐环节，导游还要适时引导旅游者文明用餐、使用公筷公勺，提倡节约，反对浪费。

026. What kind of services can you offer after the meal?（旅游者用餐后，导游应提供什么服务？）

★ Collect the feedback from the tourists and present it to the restaurant.

★ Settle accounts or sign the bill after the meal.

★ Remind tourists of their personal belongings.

☆ 收集旅游者用餐意见并反馈给餐厅。

☆ 结算费用或签单。

☆ 提醒旅游者带好随身物品。

【备注】用餐时，如遇客流量大，可提醒旅游者合理安排去洗手间的时间：用餐后去洗手间，通常排队等待时间较长，可考虑在餐前、餐中前往。当然，在餐前、餐中前往，旅游者可能会担心菜量无法保证。特别提醒：如考题关于就餐服务，则答案包括餐前、餐中和餐后三个部分；如考题关于用餐时服务，则按要求回答相关部分。务必根据考题准确作答。

027. What will you do when a tourist has special dietary requirements for religious or health reasons?（如旅游者因健康或宗教原因提出特殊用餐要求，导游应如何处理？）

★ Coordinate with the restaurant staff and try to meet his/her request due to religious or health reasons.

★ If his/her request cannot be met, help him/her order something different after he/she agrees to pay extra.

★ Try to arrange for the tourists in the following meals.

☆ 事先与餐厅协商，尽量满足其因健康、宗教原因提出的特殊用餐要求。

☆ 如果无法满足，在旅游者同意支付额外费用后，协助其点其他餐。

☆ 在后续的用餐安排中尽量协助满足。

【备注】如合同中写明旅游者为素食者，通常餐厅会为素食者单独准备一两道素食；上菜时，导游应协助说明。目前饭店给旅游者准备的素菜一般是绿色蔬菜，其中青菜居多，或是豆腐。外国人的素食种类分得很细，如 Vegan（完全素食），Ovo-Lacto Vegetarian（除蛋、奶外完全素食，也是最常见的素食），Pescetarian（除了鱼之外完全素食）等。

028. What are you going to do when you find some tourists are allergic to certain food such as seafood or MSG?（如发现旅游者对海鲜、味精等食物过敏，导游应如何处理？）

★ Once you find tourists are allergic to certain food or MSG, let the restaurant know right away because it might give rise to serious consequences.

★ Let the remaining restaurants know right away.

★ Double check if the special requirements have been fulfilled in each restaurant.

☆ 一旦得知旅游者对某种食物或味精过敏，应立即通知餐厅给予特别关照，因为有些食物和味精会引起旅游者的严重过敏，造成严重后果。

☆ 将此事通知其余该团将使用的餐厅。

☆ 在后续的餐厅用餐时，再次确认。

【备注】部分西方旅游者在进食含味精的食物、某些带壳海鲜或坚果两小时内，会出现头痛、面红、多汗、胃部烧灼感及胸痛等症状。相对而言，欧美旅游者过敏原较多，如麸质过敏（大麦、小麦、燕麦、面粉）、乳糖不耐受、甲壳类海鲜过敏、坚果过敏、豆制品过敏等。中东地区不少儿童对豆制品过敏。一般旅游者在参团时会明确告知自己的过敏原。所以，旅游者的过敏原一般会在行程单中注明，细心的旅游者会另外自备小卡片，上面写着中英文，如“我对葱/鸡蛋/芝麻/花生过敏”，便于就餐时服务员了解。如旅游者自由活动期间需要自行进餐，导游了解情况后，可以帮助旅游者制作小卡片。

029. What are you going to do when tourists want to buy and eat some local snacks sold by peddlers at scenic spots?（当旅游者想品尝景区小贩出售的小吃时，导游应如何处理？）

★ Respect their choices; remind them to check the hygiene of the stalls; discourage them from eating anything at small and unclean restaurants.

★ Tell tourists that the agency may arrange for them to sample local snacks in designated restaurants after they agree to pay extra.

☆ 尊重旅游者的选择；但要提醒旅游者关注食品卫生情况，不要在不卫生的小饭店进食。

☆ 告知旅游者，如同意支付额外费用，旅行社将协助安排在定点饭店品尝地方小吃。

【备注】“民以食为天”，旅游六要素中“食”排在第一位，可见“食”的重要性。旅游中，“食”关乎地方文化传播与品位享受。但对于身体较弱、年纪较大的旅游者，应告知饮食习惯差异可能带来的问题。例如，在上海豫园景区，旅游者会在品尝南翔小笼的时候喝矿泉水，此类情况容易引发肠胃不适，带来不必要的麻烦。

030. What will you do if tourists show symptoms of food poisoning?（如旅游者出现食物中毒症状，导游应如何处理？）

★ Ask them to drink a lot of water and if necessary ask them to take an emetic to induce vomiting.

★ Send them to the nearest hospital.

★ Report the case to the office immediately.

★ Get a medical certificate (for insurance claims).

★ After the cause has been worked out, have the tour leader or your manager make it known to the whole group.

★ Keep a record.

☆ 让旅游者大量喝水，必要时积极催吐。

☆ 就近送医。

☆ 报告旅行社。

☆ 获取医院证明（以备后续举证保险索赔）。

☆ 弄清原因后，请领队或旅行社经理告知旅游者。

☆ 做好记录。

【备注】《旅游法》第八十一条规定：突发事件或者旅游安全事故发生后，旅游经营者应当立即采取必要的救助和处置措施，依法履行报告义务，并对旅游者做出妥善安排。（According to Article 81 of Tourism Law: Immediately after an emergency or tourism safety incident, tourism operators shall take necessary assistance and settlement measures, perform the reporting obligation, and properly settle the tourists.）

031. What will you do if one of the tourists requests to dine separately due to various reasons such as conflicts with other tourists?（如因旅游者之间发生矛盾或其他原因导致个别旅游者提出要单独用餐，导游应如何处理？）

★ Try to persuade the tourist to have dinner with the group.

★ Ask the tour leader to talk with the tourist.

★ Explain to the tourist that there is no refund on unused meals. Also additional charges for further arrangement are to be covered by the tourist.

★ If the tourist still insists and agrees to pay, the tour guide may help contact the restaurant.

☆ 导游要尽力劝说其与其他旅游者一起进餐。

☆ 告诉领队请其调解。

☆ 告知旅游者原餐费不退，额外安排发生的费用由旅游者自理。

☆ 如果旅游者依然坚持要求单独用餐并同意支付额外费用，导游可协助其与餐厅联系。

【备注】涉及点餐的费用，请旅游者现付。通常的支付原则是“谁提出，谁支付”。

032. What will you do if tourists suggest sampling some special dishes at another restaurant just before mealtime?（如在即将用餐时，旅游者提出更换餐厅品尝特色菜肴，导游应如何处理？）

★ Politely refuse his request as changing the restaurant in such a short notice would be very inconvenient.

★ Explain the reason for your refusal patiently.

★ Help arrange for the tourist in following days.

★ If extra money is concerned, tell tourists and collect money in advance.

☆ 因即将用餐，换餐厅非常麻烦，故礼貌拒绝。

☆ 耐心解释，赢得理解。

☆ 在后续用餐安排中协助落实。

☆ 如涉及额外费用，提前告知旅游者并收取费用。

Related words and phrases

serving chopsticks	公筷
buffet	自助餐
banquet	宴会
Western food	西餐
Chinese food	中餐
specialty dish	特色菜
cold dish	冷菜
home dish/home-cooked dish	家常菜

country-style cuisine	农家菜
local snacks	地方小吃
Chinese salad	凉拌菜
set meal	套餐
eight dishes with a soup	八菜一汤
Chinese herbal cuisine	中国药膳
Chinese white spirit/*bai jiu*	白酒
Chinese yellow wine/*huang jiu*	黄酒
chrysanthemum tea	菊花茶
oolong tea	乌龙茶
jasmine tea	茉莉花茶
Monosodium glutamate (MSG)	味精

Questions for discussion

1. What will you do if a tourist feels sick due to contaminated food?
2. What kind of information are you going to provide to tourists before you take them to a famous restaurant (for Beijing roast duck)?
3. How will you assist tourists who are feeling unwell and prefer a simple and light meal?

听力音频

Unit 5 Sightseeing 游览服务

033. How will you organize visiting activities properly for a day?（导游应如何安排一天的行程？）

When organizing visiting activities for a day, the tour guide should pay attention to the following aspects:

★ Make good use of time. (For example, the tour guide may choose a short-cut if the main traffic is heavy. He/She should figure out the most reasonable schedule in order not to waste time on the way.)

★ Special attention should also be paid to sequences of activities. (For example, usually the guide should take tourists to the farthest place first, and then take them to a place which is closer to the hotel. Besides, he/she should avoid taking the same way, for different routine may bring tourists different experience.)

★ Well arrange different kinds of activities. (Different kinds of sceneries and activities will make tourists full of interests and energy. For example, shopping tour should not be arranged more than twice in a day. Or if tourists are tired after climbing a mountain, the guide should not arrange another mountain-climbing activity on the same day.)

安排一天的行程时，导游应注意以下几点：

☆ 合理安排时间，旅速游缓（缩短旅途中时间，选择最佳旅游路线，避开拥堵路段）。

☆ 先后有序（先远后近、先高后低、渐入佳境、不走回头路）。

☆ 错落有致（不同旅游景观结合、不同活动内容结合）。

【备注】本题因情况不同往往有不同的理解。如某些高品质团队，组团社明确说明在任何情况下，导游无权更改行程安排，包括项目顺序。有些项目涉及沿途观光，其行车路线也是规定的，导游不能更改。此外，导游更改项目顺序可被投诉为违反合同，且如果其间发生任何意外，导游还要承担一定的责任。基于以上种种，导游灵活安排的空间极为有限。因此本题中的灵活安排多指接团后依据客人兴趣而制定的行程安排。

034. What kind of services will you offer when tourists are getting on the bus?（旅游者登车时，导游应提供怎样的服务？）

★ If there is a stool on the coach, ask the driver to get it prepared.

★ Stand beside the gate of the coach, welcoming tourists with a smile.

★ If there are disabled or senior tourists, the guide should ask whether they need help and arrange reserved seats for them.

★ Help the driver with tourists' wheelchairs if there are any.

☆ 如大巴车司机备有矮凳，请司机提前放置（以便于腿脚不便的旅游者登车）。

☆ 站在车门旁，面带微笑欢迎旅游者上车。

☆ 如有腿脚不便或年纪大的旅游者，主动询问登车时是否需要帮助，并安排其坐在前排预留位置。

☆ 如有旅游者携带轮椅，协助司机安放。

【备注】导游在接团准备期间，可提前制作“预留座位”的卡片，为年纪大或是活动不便的旅游者预留出前排座位。提前标识“导游专座”，以避免旅游者坐定后更换座位。2016 年 4 月发布的《关于进一步规范导游专座等有关事宜的通知》中规定：“导游专座”是指旅游客运车辆在提供旅游服务时，为导游人员设置的专用座位。“导游专座”设置在旅游客运车辆前乘客门侧第一排乘客座椅靠通道侧位置。

035. What will you remind tourists before they get off the coach for a tour?（旅游者下车游览前，导游应关照哪些事宜？）

★ Let tourists know the way you conduct the tour. (For example: Is it a guided tour and how to keep people together? If there is a group banner, what does it look like? How fast is your pace? What to expect? Will the tour be indoors or outdoors? Is there much walking? Are there many stairs and how much time they will have to take photos?)

★ Point out the tour sign placed in the front of the coach or its license plate number.

★ Remind them to take care of their personal belongings.

★ Tell tourists the meeting time and place.

☆ 告知旅游者你带团游览的方式。（比如是否有讲解，怎样做到不掉队？如果使用导游旗，它有什么特点？你行走的速度是快还是慢？路上可能会出现什么样的情况？景点是室内还是室外？到景点需要走多长时间的路？景点是否有许多台阶？景点拍照如何安排等？）

☆ 向旅游者示意车前旅游标识或车牌号。

☆ 提醒旅游者看管好随身物品。

☆ 告知旅游者集合时间和地点。

【备注】导游在提供服务时，应规范使用导游旗。避免使用过多或造型怪异的挂饰，以免影响导游旗的正常使用和辨识。当旅游者人数超过 10 人时，必须用导游旗。保持旗杆直立，旗面位于旅游者容易辨识的位置。暂时不使用导游旗时，应妥善放置，以维护其专业形象。

036. What will you remind tourists before starting a tour in a scenic spot?（游览景点前，导游应关照哪些事宜？）

★ Emphasize the duration of the tour, departure time and the meeting point.

★ If entry and exit are in two different places, make it known to the whole group.

★ Give a brief introduction to the spot.

★ Emphasize safety precautions.

☆ 强调此景点需用多长时间以及何时离开、集中地点。

☆ 如出入口不在同一处，提醒旅游者，以防走失。

☆ 简要介绍景点。

☆ 景区游览的注意事项。

【**备注**】本题与前一题容易混淆，前一题的前提是旅游者依然在车上；本题的前提是旅游者已经下车并在景区门口。重要信息如集合时间和地点、安全注意事项在这两题中都需要强调。景区游览注意事项：如在景区特设场景拍照是否收费；与特色人物或动物拍照是否收费；景区内如有小商贩叫卖A货，应如何处理等。另，需再次确认旅游者知晓导游的联系方式。

037. What will you do when you find a tourist missing after free-time activity?（自由活动结束后，如发现一位旅游者未按时归队，导游应如何处理？）

★ Try to contact the tourist. If the tourist gets lost, tell him/her to stay where he/she is, and the tour leader or guide will come to assist him/her.

★ Wait for another 15 minutes to see whether he/she will show up or contact you. The tour guide may consider using the public address system to look for the tourist.

★ If someone is late, give him/her a hint in a humorous way. Don't shame him/her in front of the whole group.

★ If you still cannot find him/her after 15 minutes, continue the tour.

★ The tour leader, together with the national guide and the tourist's relatives may continue looking for the tourist.

★ Keep in touch with the hotel and make sure that they will let you know after the tourist is back.

★ If you fail to find the tourist, report the case to the travel agency and the police.

☆ 主动联系旅游者，如旅游者迷失方向，请他/她原地不动，领队或全陪前去接应。

☆ 如无法联系，原地等候 15 分钟，看看旅游者是否会联系导游或能赶到，必要时可请景区广播找人。

☆ 如旅游者迟到，应以幽默、睿智的方式给予暗示，不要当众责备旅游者。
☆ 如旅游者 15 分钟后仍未归队，地陪继续带团游览。
☆ 领队、全陪和走失旅游者亲友留下继续寻找。
☆ 与酒店保持联系，一有旅游者消息就通知你。
☆ 如旅游者一直未找到，向旅行社报告并报警。

【备注】为方便旅游者走失后能够与地陪取得联系，或自行返回酒店，地陪应及时为旅游者提供酒店名片，并将自己的手机号码告知旅游者。

038. What type of sanitary facilities are preferred by tourists in a tourist spot?（旅游者对景点卫生设施有什么要求？）

★ Not all people have the same level of acceptance for sanitary facilities. Common complaints and grievances about restrooms include: Some restrooms do not provide toilet paper, hand sanitizer, or hand-dryers; Some restrooms do not have seated toilets; Some restrooms do not have partitions at all; And the ventilation in some restrooms is poor, with unpleasant odors in the air.

★ Tourists generally have the following requirements for restrooms: cleanliness, well-equipped facilities (especially toilet paper and seated toilets), good ventilation, and privacy protection.

★ Take tourists to the cleanest washroom with more seated toilets.

☆ 旅游者对卫生设施有不同的标准和要求。（外国游客）对于厕所常见的抱怨和投诉有：没有提供厕纸、洗手液、干手器等；没有坐便设施；没有隔断；通风条件较差，空气有异味。

☆ 旅游者对洗手间通常期待如下：清洁、设施完备（尤其是厕纸和坐便器）、通风良好并且具有隐私保护设施。

☆ 导游应尽量安排旅游者去卫生条件好的、有坐式设施的厕所。

【备注】对旅游者而言，洗手间卫生情况不仅可以满足基本生理需求，还影响旅游体验，同时体现景区管理水平和服务质量。“上知天文地理，下知厕所距离”曾用来形容导游的知识结构。在实际工作中，尤其是接待国外旅游者时，导游会发现仅仅知晓这些还不够。洗手间是蹲式的还是坐式的，是否有手纸，有几个位置，哪个洗手间最干净等，都是服务中需要知晓并告知旅游者的。

039. Are there better ways that guides can share with tourists to take good care of their passports, money and valuables?（如何能使旅游者更好地保管好自己的护照、现金及其他贵重物品？）

★ Most tourists know that they should take care of their own valuable belongings.

★ Make sure they get their passports back after scanning

on the first day when they check in at the hotel.

★ Kindly suggest that they leave behind their passports, big-denomination cash, jewelry and other valuable things in a safe place at the hotel before they go out for a tour.

★ On the tour, remind them to keep an eye on their own valuable things, especially in the crowded places.

★ When they get off coach for meals, make sure that they have their valuable things with them and do not leave them on the coach.

☆ 多数旅游者清楚他们自己应保管好随身物品。

☆ 在办理入住酒店手续时，护照扫描后应尽快还给旅游者。

☆ 建议旅游者在游览前将护照、大额现金、珠宝及其他贵重物品留在酒店妥善保管。

☆ 提醒旅游者在游览中，尤其在人群拥挤处，照看好随身物品。

☆ 下车用餐时，提醒旅游者将贵重物品随身携带，不要留在旅游车里。

040. What assistance will you provide during tourists' free time?（旅游者自由活动时，导游应做好哪些协助工作？）

★ Remind them to take the hotel card with them.

★ Ask them not to visit remote places or places which are not safe and remind them to take care of themselves and their personal belongings.
★ If it is needed, help arrange cars or taxis for them.
★ Remind them not to return to the hotel too late.
★ Tell them in advance that all extra expense is to be covered by themselves.

☆ 旅游者离开饭店时，导游有必要提醒他们带上饭店联系卡。
☆ 提醒旅游者不要走得太远，也不要去治安不好的地方，照顾好自己及随身物品。
☆ 若有需要还应帮助旅游者安排车辆（费用自理）。
☆ 提醒旅游者不要太晚回宾馆。
☆ 由此发生的费用由旅游者自理。

【备注】《旅游法》第七十条规定：在旅游者自行安排活动期间，旅行社未尽到安全提示、救助义务的，应当对旅游者的人身损害、财产损失承担相应责任。(According to Article 70 of *Tourism Law*: The travel agency shall bear corresponding responsibility for any personal damage or property loss caused to the tourists in free time because of the travel agency's failure to fully fulfill its obligation of giving safety warnings or offering assistance.)

041. What are the special circumstances in which the tour guide should discourage free activities of tourists?（导游应劝阻旅游者自由活动的特殊情况有哪些？）

★ The group is about to leave the city.

★ Tourists are going to certain areas that are not open to foreigners.

★ Tourists are going to places which are chaotic or not safe.

★ Tourists are going to participate in activities that are either insecure or illegal.

☆ 旅游团即将离开本地时。

☆ 旅游者提出要去不对外开放的区域。

☆ 旅游者要去的地方治安情况不好。

☆ 旅游者要去参加有潜在不安全因素的活动或不合法的活动。

【备注】导游在劝阻旅游者自由活动时，应耐心解释，说清理由和利害关系，切忌危言耸听、简单粗暴地回绝。

042. What are you supposed to do on the way back to hotel when the group has finished all programs of the day?（在结束一天的行程回酒店的途中，导游应提供哪些服务？）

★ Make a brief conclusion of the day's activities, answer

questions if there are any.

★ Show tourists beautiful scenery and impressive buildings along the road.

★ Tell tourists the schedule of the next day.

☆ 回顾当天旅游活动，询问旅游者感受，回答旅游者提问。

☆ 沿途风光导游。

☆ 宣布次日活动日程（包括次日行程、出发时间、天气预报等）。

Related words and phrases

tourist attractions	旅游胜地
remains of ancient culture	文化遗址
eco-tourism	生态旅游
national geo-park	地质公园
game sanctuary	野生动物保护区
theme park	主题公园
state-listed famous historic and cultural cities	国家历史文化名城
seaside resort	海滨疗养胜地
summer resort	避暑胜地
hot spring resort	温泉度假地
national nature reserve	国家自然保护区
holiday villa	度假村
places of historical interest	历史古迹
golden cities	旅游热点城市

Questions for discussion

1. What are you going to say shortly before people get off the coach for a tour of Summer Palace?
2. As a local tour guide, what measures can you take to avoid losing tourists in sightseeing spots?

听力音频

Unit 6 Transportation 交通服务

043. How will you deal with a serious traffic accident?（如何处理严重交通事故？）

★ Once it happens, stay calm; take immediate measures to rescue the wounded.

★ Call 110, 120, 122 and ask for help; report the case to the agency.

★ Stay with the rest of the tourists and help them to calm down.

★ Get involved in the investigation of the traffic accident.

★ Share the cause of the accident with the whole group once it is made clear.

★ Keep a record.

☆ 一旦发生此类事件，保持冷静，迅速采取行动救助伤者。

☆ 联系 110、120、122 寻求紧急救援，向旅行社报告。

☆ 与旅游者待在一起，并尽量安抚他们。

☆ 积极参与交通事故的调查。

☆ 一旦查明事故原因，及时告知全团旅游者。

☆ 做好事件记录备案。

【备注】 122报警服务台是公安交通管理机关为受理群众交通事故报警电话，指挥调度警员处理各种报警、求助、同时受理群众对交通管理和交通民警执法问题的举报、投诉、查询等而设的部门。该部门是公安交通管理机关指挥中心的主要组成部分。如在高速公路上发生车祸，导游应组织旅游者迅速转移到安全地带，以避免车祸后的连锁反应，导致更大的事故、财产损失或人员伤亡。

044. What will you do to guarantee the safety of the group when the group is traveling by coach?（乘汽车旅行途中，为保障旅游者和自身安全，导游应做些什么？）

★ Make sure the luggage is well placed; No luggage or other obstacles can be stacked along the aisle.

★ Remind tourists of safety precautions, such as not extending hands or heads out of the windows; remaining seated when the coach is moving; fastening the seat belts.

★ Remind the driver not to exceed the speed limit. Before departure, communicate with the driver about the route, parking site, meeting place, etc. Avoiding interfering the driver when he is driving.

★ Sit in the reserved seat for tour guides. Do not stand and give explanations when the coach is driving on the highway or in dangerous areas.

☆ 检查行李架，将行李安全放置；车内通道不得堆放行李和其他障碍物。

☆ 提醒旅游者安全注意事项，如：不要将手、头等伸出窗外；在车辆行驶过程中不要随意走动；系好安全带等。

☆ 提醒司机安全行车不要超速；在车辆启动之前与司机充分沟通行车路线、停靠站点、上车集合点等；避免在行车过程中影响司机正常驾驶。

☆ 导游在“导游专座”就座；车辆在高速公路或危险路段行驶时，导游不应站立讲解。

【备注】2016年4月国家旅游局和交通运输部两部委共同发布了《关于进一步规范导游专座等有关事宜的通知》（旅发〔2016〕51号），以下简称《通知》）。《通知》规定：①旅游客运企业在旅游服务过程中，应配备印有“导游专座”字样的座套；②旅游客运企业应督促司机严格遵守道路交通安全和道路运输管理法律法规，不超员、不超速，安全文明驾驶，行车之前播放《游客安全乘车温馨提示》宣传片；③车内通道不得堆放行李和其他障碍物，逃生装置要定期维护、标识清晰，确保正常使用；④逾期未予整改的旅行社，旅游客运企业可以拒绝为其提供服务。

调查数据显示：在一次可能导致死亡的车祸中，安全带的使用可使车内人员生还的概率提高60%。发生正面撞车时，系上安全带可使死亡率减少57%；侧面撞车时可减少死亡率44%；翻车时可减少死亡率80%。依据2017年新交通法，乘车人不按规定系安全带也要受到相应的处罚。

本题由四个小点组成，分别是关于行李、旅游者、司机和导游自身。

045. What help can you offer to those who are likely to suffer from carsickness?（对易晕车的旅游者，导游可以提供哪些服务？）

★ Remind them not to eat too much, not to eat greasy or oily food, not to drink alcohol.

★ Remind them not to play with cell phones or read books.

★ Remind them to take dramamine/carsick medicine before boarding.

★ Arrange window seats for them.

★ Keep the air of the coach fresh.

★ Offer plastic bags for them.

☆ 提醒容易晕车的旅游者，登车前不宜吃太饱，不宜吃油腻食品，不宜饮酒。

☆ 提醒旅游者不玩手机、不看书。

☆ 提醒旅游者上车前服用晕车药。

☆ 为其安排靠窗位置。

☆ 保持车厢内空气清新。

☆ 提供塑料袋以备用。

【备注】本题的答题要点主要包括三个提醒和三个预防措施。

046. What will you do if someone vomits on the coach?（如旅游者在车上呕吐，导游应如何处理？）

★ Offer a plastic bag to him/her right away.

★ Work with the driver as a team to stop and evacuate the coach where possible. Open all the doors and windows to ventilate the coach.

★ Clean the coach before tourists get on board again.

☆ 立即提供塑料袋。

☆ 让司机在安全、适当的地方停车，请旅游者下车，开门窗通风。

☆ 清理污物后，再让旅游者登车。

【备注】笔者就此问题做过调研，目前清理工作没有明确规定的操作形式。调研反馈中，有司机清理的，有导游清理的，有导游协同司机清理的，有通情达理的旅游者家属协助司机清理的，也有旅游者出少量清理费的解决案例。通常旅游者（尤其是西方旅游者）会通过多给小费的形式表示感谢。为避免此类情况的发生，预防工作要到位。

047. What will you do to win cooperation of tourists when your group is stuck in a traffic jam?（如何让旅游者在遇到堵车时心平气和，并接受由此可能带来的游览时间的变化？）

★ In big cities like Shanghai, you may talk about traffic jam of the city with the whole group in advance.

★ You may tell tourists by saying: "As we know, Shanghai is a busy city. The traffic is often very heavy, especially during rush hours. According to the latest statistics, Shanghai is one of the most crowded cities in the world. So if we are held up in the traffic jam, please be patient. But if there is no traffic jam during the whole tour, we shall be very lucky. Probably it may save us a lot of time."

★ In most cases, if the group is caught in a traffic jam, tourists won't complain.

☆ 大城市堵车是常见的现象。在诸如上海这样的大城市，导游可以主动跟旅游者介绍城市交通状况。

☆ 导游可以这么说："上海是个交通繁忙的城市，尤其是在上下班高峰期。最新数据显示，上海是全球最拥堵城市之一。所以，如果我们遇到堵车，请大家不要着急；如果我们很幸运一路顺畅，我们也会因此节省不少时间。"

☆ 多数情况下，如遭遇堵车，旅游者会理解并配合。

【备注】在诸如上海这样的大城市，交通的通畅与否常常会导致游览时间的变化。因交通状况而带来的行程提前或延后结束是常见的现象，因此提前与旅游者交流这一问题，有助于后续可能出现的此类情况。此外，预先准备一两个专题讲解，对缓解堵车时旅游者的情绪很有帮助。

048. What will you do to drop a mild hint to tourists who keep talking loudly when you are giving presentation on the coach?（在车上讲解时，有旅游者大声喧哗影响讲解效果，导游应如何处理？）

★ Good presentation speaks for itself. Always improve yourself, especially your tour presentation.

★ You may either say, "I am sorry that I did not speak loud enough, so I am afraid that guests on the back rows could not hear me. Okay, now, can guests in the back hear me?"

★ Or you may say with a smile, "I am afraid that some of you are not so interested in this topic. Okay, I'd like to share with you some interesting stories about the city."

★ If some tourists still keep talking, you may say, "And gentlemen there, what do you want to know about the city?"

★ In this way, you may probably drop a hint while "saving their faces".

☆ 好的讲解自然会吸引旅游者。不断提升自己，提高自己的讲解水平。

☆ 你可以跟旅游者说："对不起，刚才可能我讲话的声音太小，所以使得后面的客人听不清楚。接下来，我声音大一些，请问后面的客人能听到吗？"

☆ 你也可以边微笑边说："对不起，可能刚才的讲解有些客人不感兴趣，这样吧，我讲一些大家感兴趣的内容。"

☆ 如旅游者依然我行我素，你可以说："嗯，后面的几位客人希望我讲些什么内容呢？"

☆ 这样的回应，既没有损害旅游者的面子，又可以阻止他们大声喧哗。

【备注】导游讲解并非越多越好，导游应根据旅游者的实际情况，或讲解，或安排娱乐活动，或让旅游者休息。

Related words and phrases

Dramamine	茶苯海明（晕车药）
evacuate	疏散
fracture	骨折
be rear-ended	被追尾
a cold compress pack/ice pack	冰袋
underpass	地下通道
safety island	安全岛
pedestrian crossing	斑马线

avenue	大道
turnstile	入口处旋转式栅门
revolving door	转闸
to punch a hole in a ticket	检票打孔
platform ticket	站台票
same-day validity ticket	当天有效票
luggage rack	行李架
upper/lower berth	上/下铺
hard berth	硬卧
to refund a ticket	退票
scooter	小型摩托车
no honking	禁止鸣喇叭

Questions for discussion

1. What will you do when someone gets injured in a car accident and has to be hospitalized just before the group leaves for another city?
2. What are you going to do when the group gets stuck in a traffic jam on the way to a scenic spot?

听力音频

Unit 7 Shopping and Entertainment 购物与文化娱乐服务

049. What is considered a good shopping tour?（愉快的购物活动应具备什么特点？）

★ Tourists enjoy a good shopping experience (good environment and service; no pressure to purchase).

★ Tourists are satisfied with the purchase (good quality at a reasonable price and with local features).

☆ 旅游者享受购物过程（环境舒适、服务周到、无强制购物）。

☆ 旅游者对所购之物感到满意（物美价廉、富有特色）。

【备注】《旅游法》第三十五条规定：旅行社组织、接待旅游者，不得指定具体购物场所。但是，经双方协商一致或者旅游者要求，且不影响其他旅游者行程安排的除外。(According to Article 35 of *Tourism Law*: When organizing and receiving tourists, travel agencies shall not designate specific shopping places, or provide tourism services that require additional payment. However, it does not include circumstances where both sides have agreed or the tourists have requested for such arrangements and no influence is caused on the itinerary of other tourists.)

050. What advice and services will you provide to tourists before a shopping expedition?（旅游者购物前，导游应提供哪些服务和建议？）

★ Give them a friendly reminder (taking care of their personal belongings including passports and valuables).

★ Recommend unique gifts and souvenirs honestly.

★ Suggest that they ask for formal receipts for major purchases.

★ Suggest that they compare the price of items with that of similar ones at home to see whether it is worth buying and try to bargain.

★ Announce an appointed time and place for regrouping.

☆ 提醒旅游者保管好护照及贵重物品。

☆ 如实推荐特色旅游纪念品。

☆ 如购买贵重物品，建议旅游者索要正规发票。

☆ 建议旅游者可参照所在国同类物品的价格，理性购物，不忘还价。

☆ 宣布集合时间和地点。

【备注】如无须在银行兑换货币，旅游者可将护照存放在宾馆保险箱；购物时，用护照复印件亦可。在免税店或特定的退税商店，导游应提前提醒旅游者相关的退税政策。

051. What should you do on a shopping tour?（旅游者购物时，导游应注意哪些问题？）

★ Don't stay away from tourists in case they need help.

★ Don't hover and give them space but be nearby.

★ Never get yourself involved in bargaining.

★ If something unpleasant happens, try to solve the problem in the interests of the tourists.

☆ 不要远离旅游者，以便提供帮助（如旅游者不熟悉当地语言或文化，导游可以协助沟通，避免因语言或文化差异造成误解或不愉快的购物体验）。

☆ 不要紧跟着旅游者，给旅游者自由购物的空间。

☆ 不要参与还价。

☆ 购物过程中如有不愉快事件发生，遵循旅游者利益至上的原则进行处理。

【备注】本题的答题思路是"不远、不近、不还价、不回避"。"不还价"指不参与还价，"不回避"指出现问题时主动积极解决。

052. What should you do when some tourists want to buy traditional Chinese medicine?（如旅游者想购买中药，导游如何处理比较妥当？）

★ Recommend reliable drugstores to tourists.

★ Inform tourists in advance about the relevant regulations for carrying traditional Chinese medicine out of Chinese mainland. (For example, inform tourists there is a limit to the amount of Chinese medicines one can take out of Chinese mainland for personal use: tourists bound for foreign countries are allowed to carry no more than RMB 300 yuan's worth of traditional Chinese medicines and patent drugs; those bound for Hong Kong, Macao and Taiwan no more than RMB 150 yuan. Items such as musk, rhinoceros horn and tiger bone are prohibited to be taken out of country.)

☆ 了解需求，推荐可靠的药店。

☆ 提前告知旅游者关于携带中草药出境的相关法规。（如告知旅游者，海关对旅客携带个人使用中药材、中成药离开中国内地的限制政策：旅客携带中药材、中成药出境前往国外的总值限人民币 300 元，前往港澳台地区的总值限人民币 150 元。麝香、犀牛角、虎骨等不准携带出境。）

【备注】近年来，中药中医为越来越多的国外旅游者所了解，对此导游应提前做好功课。导游可将有需要的旅游者带到一些著名旅游景点内的知名药店，如在上海豫园景区有诸如“童涵春堂”之类的药房，药房内有坐诊医师，也有会简单英文的工作人员。

053. What should you do when some tourists want to buy antiques?（如旅游者想购买文物古董，导游如何处理比较妥当？）

★ Tell tourists when they are buying antiques, they should

be cautious and never buy antiques sold by peddlers or small shops.

★ Recommend reliable antique shops to tourists.

★ Remind them to ask for official receipts.

★ Inform tourists in advance about the relevant regulations for carrying antiques out of the country. (For example, inform tourists cultural relics/antiques eligible for legal export must have a "wax seal" and complete documentation. Additionally, those from before 1911 are prohibited from being exported.)

☆ 告知旅游者，购买文物古董需谨慎，切勿在路边或小店购买。

☆ 为旅游者推荐可靠的商店。

☆ 提醒旅游者购买文物古董时索要正规发票。

☆ 提前告知旅游者关于携带文物古董出境的相关法规。（如告知旅游者，可以合法出境的文物应有"火漆印"，且手续齐全；1911 年以前的文物禁止出境等。）

【备注】"火漆印"标志是中国文物出境的专用章，文物可否出境的标志是文物上是否有"火漆印"。中国海关对海外旅客购买文物有如下规定：携带在合法的文物商店购买的文物的旅客应向海关申报。作为礼品或在自由市场上购买的文物，应提供北京、天津、上海或广州的海关检验文化管理部门签发的专用章和发票，海关将根据鉴定标志和许可出口证明放行。

054. What kind of services will you provide for entertainment program?（导游应如何做好文化娱乐服务？）

★ Try to learn something about the program and give a brief introduction to the program.

★ Tell tourists the meeting time and place.

★ Remind tourists to take care of themselves and their personal belongings.

★ Help with seating the tourists.

★ For outdoor programs, the guide should keep an eye on tourists and surroundings.

★ On the way back, review the program and answer questions if there are any.

☆ 应预先了解娱乐项目内容，向旅游者简单介绍节目内容和特点。

☆ 告知旅游者观赏结束后的集合时间和地点。

☆ 提醒旅游者注意自身安全并保管好个人财物。

☆ 引导旅游者入座。

☆ 如是室外娱乐活动，注意旅游者动向和周围环境，以防不测。

☆ 在演出结束后的回程途中，导游要向旅游者作节目回顾，解答旅游者的提问。

【备注】如在大型文娱场所观看演出，演出介绍、集合时间、地点、观看须知等信息需在车上提前讲清。

055. If tourists ask to change the theatrical performance in the itinerary to another show, how will you deal with it?（如合同中已安排观看文艺演出，旅游者却要求替换观看另一演出，导游应如何处理？）

★ If time permits and the program is possible to be changed, you can ask the travel agency to help you with the change.

★ If the tourists insist on watching another show, you may offer assistance, but you should tell them that they are responsible for extra expense and the original performance cannot be refunded.

★ Ask tourists to sign their names on related forms.

★ If it cannot be arranged due to various reasons, you should explain patiently.

☆ 如果时间许可又有可能调换，可请旅行社出面调换。

☆ 若旅游者坚持要求观看别的演出，导游可协助，但费用自理，原费用不退。

☆ 请旅游者留下书面说明材料。

☆ 如无法安排，导游要作耐心解释，请其谅解。

056. What will you do when some tourists think a silk carpet is expensive and ask for your advice?（如旅游者想购买地毯，却因价格较高而向导游咨询，导游应如何处理？）

★ Do not suggest tourists to buy or not to buy anything.

★ Tell them to buy those which they will not regret for.

★ Remind them to compare prices and quality, but never help bargain.

★ You may tell tourists "The silk carpet is a kind of traditional commodity. As a kind of handicraft, it is made of different materials and it may have various traditional patterns. Even if they are made of the same material and have the same pattern, they may be of different quality and craftsmanship. And as I said before, since it is a kind of handicraft, different producers may have their own styles, thus different prices. But, since you are interested in silk carpets, I do hope that you may get what you want after comparing the prices, quality and details."

☆ 不要建议旅游者买或不买某样商品。

☆ 告诉他们买他们不会后悔的商品。

☆ 提醒旅游者比较价格质量，但不要协助还价。

☆ 你可以跟旅游者这么说："地毯是传统的工艺品，它讲究材质、构图等元素。作为工艺品，即使材质图案相同，质量和工艺也可能有所差异。工艺品由于生产厂家不同，风格也不尽相同，这也有可能造成价格上的差异。您既然对地毯感兴趣，我希望您在考虑以上因素的基础上决定是否需要购买。”

057. How should a tour guide deal with the case that a tourist finds the necklace bought in the designated shop is of inferior quality?（如旅游者发现在定点商店购买的项链有质量问题，要求退货，导游应如何处理？）

★ Figure out details of the case.

★ Offer timely help and accompany the tourist to the shop, negotiating with the shop if necessary.

★ If the shop refuses to refund or change a new one for the tourist, you can contact the travel agency, asking for help from local tourism administrative departments for help.

☆ 了解具体情况。

☆ 积极协助，必要时陪同交涉退货事宜。

☆ 如商家拒绝退赔，可联系旅行社请相关部门协助解决。

Related words and phrases

flea market	跳蚤市场
junk shop/market	旧货商店/市场
special local products	地方特产

feather fan	羽毛扇
wooden crafts/wood carvings	木雕
Chinese traditional kite craft	中国风筝工艺
Chinese papercut	剪纸
Chinese knot	中国结
Jingtailan/cloisonné	景泰蓝
Han/Tang-Dynasty attire	汉服/唐服
Chinese Qipao/Cheongsam	旗袍/长衫
costumes of ethnic minorities in China	民族服饰
after-sales service	售后服务
high-quality goods	优质商品
cultured pearls	人工养殖珍珠
ask for a receipt/invoice	索要收据/发票
bargain	超值物品；讨价还价
consignment piece	托付物
Museum of Arts and Crafts	工艺美术博物馆
Alipay	支付宝
WeChat Pay	微信支付

Questions for discussion

1. What responsibilities should a tour guide bear when he/she takes tourists to go shopping?
2. What would you do if a jade bracelet bought by a tourist is proved to be deceptively misrepresented?
3. A tourist intends to buy some ancient Chinese calligraphy. What should a tour guide advise him/her to do?

听力音频

Unit 8 Hotel Check-out and Departure 离店与送站服务

058. What preparation should be made to ensure that the group leaves for the next stop smoothly?（为了保证旅游团顺利离开本地，导游必须采取的预防措施有哪些？）

★ Carefully check details of tickets on the day before departure (the number of tickets, names, date, flight, airports, port of destination).

★ Double-check the above information on the day of departure. (Pay special attention to departure time especially when a new timetable is replacing the old one.)

★ Well arrange the departure (leaving enough time for packing, cooperating with the driver) and make sure the group arrive at the port before the designated time.

★ Avoid arranging shopping or free activities for tourists before departure.

☆ 离站前一天仔细核对离站的交通票据（票据数量、姓名、日期、班次、航空港、目的港）。

☆ 离站当天再次核对。（新旧时刻表更换时，特别注意核对，以免出错。）

☆ 留出充裕的时间，注意与司机密切配合，保证旅游团按规定时间到达交通港。

☆ 临出发前不安排旅游者购物或自由活动，以免旅游者走失。

【备注】乘坐火车，若儿童身高在1.2米以下，则免票；若儿童身高为1.2~1.5米的，须购买儿童票；超过1.5米的，须购买全价票。每一成人旅客可免费携带一名身高不足1.2米的儿童；超过一名时，超过的人数应买儿童票。乘坐飞机，年龄2~12周岁的儿童，国内机票一般按照同一航班成人普通全票价的50%购买儿童票，燃油附加费收取50%，提供座位；国际机票有成人陪伴的儿童可享受成人销售价75%的价格。无成人陪伴的儿童(5~12周岁）需购买成人票，在航空公司柜台办理。年龄0~2周岁的婴儿，国内机票按照同一航班成人普通全票价的10%购买婴儿票，免燃油附加费，不提供座位；如需要单独占用座位，须购买儿童票；每一成人旅客携带婴儿超过一名时，超过的人数须购买儿童票；国际婴儿票价一般为成人全价的10%，均无座位。

059. When a group is about to leave the hotel to the next city, what services should be provided by the tour guide?（旅游团即将离开酒店赴下一城市时，导游应做哪些工作？）

★ Luggage delivery.

★ Check-out procedures.

★ Before departing make sure all tourists are on broad and remind tourists to have everything with them including passports and valuables in the safe in their rooms.

☆ 集中交运行李。

☆ 办理退房手续。

☆ 出发前，检查人数和提醒旅游者检查证件和随身携带行李，尤其是房间保险柜中是否有遗漏物品。

060. What services can a tour guide offer in order to deliver luggage smoothly when the group is leaving the hotel to the next city?（旅游团即将离开酒店赴下一城市时，导游应做哪些工作以确保行李顺利移交？）

★ Inform tourists in advance of the exact check-out time, so that they may have enough time for packing.

★ Remind tourists not to pack their valuables and required travel documents into the luggage; remind them that luggage should be locked.

★ Arrange luggage collection and count the number of pieces with the tour leader and the luggage handler.

★ Write down the number and leave them to the luggage handler.

★ If luggage goes with the coach, help with loading.

☆ 提前告知旅游者离店时间，以便他们有足够的时间打包行李。
☆ 提醒旅游者不要把贵重物品或旅行证件打包，提醒旅游者给行李上锁。
☆ 与领队、行李员共同收集行李，并清点数量。
☆ 写下行李件数后，将行李交接给行李员。
☆ 如行李随车，协助行李装车。

【备注】国内航线，一般规定头等舱旅客托运行李额为 40 千克，公务舱托运行李额为 30 千克，经济舱托运行李额度为 20 千克，婴儿票没有免费行李额。各航空公司的不同航线有不同的免费行李额，地陪 / 领队 / 全陪需熟悉所服务的团队的具体情况。

061. What do check-out procedures include?（导游办理离店手续主要包括哪些内容？）

★ Arrive at the hotel before the designated departure time, waiting in the lobby.
★ Make sure all room cards are returned.
★ All the bills including personal consumption are settled.
★ Solve problems in a smart way if there are any.

☆ 在约定离店时间之前到达宾馆，在大堂等候。
☆ 收齐房卡交还总台。
☆ 协助宾馆结清旅游者个人消费账目。
☆ 如遇到问题，灵活解决。

【备注】目前，宾馆常规退房时间为中午 12 点，但多数酒店都能灵活地办理较早入住或较晚离店的手续，具体视客户要求及酒店入住率而定。另外，导游应告知旅游者充电宝只能在手提行李中携带或随身携带，严禁在托运行李中携带。充电宝额定功率不超过 100Wh，无须航空公司批准；额定功率超过 100Wh 但不超过 160Wh，经航空公司批准后方可携带，但每名旅客不得携带两个以上充电宝；额定功率超过 160Wh，禁止携带。

062. What services can a tour guide offer to prevent the loss of luggage?（如何防止行李丢失？）

If there is a luggage handler for the group:

★ When picking up the group at the port, the tour guide should collect and count the number of the luggage with the tour leader and the luggage handler.

★ Check with the hotel the exact number of luggage, and urge the concierge to send luggage according to the rooming list in time.

★ When checking out at the hotel, once again collect and count the number of the luggage with the tour leader and the luggage handler.

If there is no luggage handler for the group:

★ The tour guide should remind tourists to take care of their own luggage.

★ Remind tourists to pay special attention to their own luggage at the traffic port or when the group is leaving the hotel for the port. And make sure all tourists see their luggage loading.

团队安排行李员的服务要点：

☆ 接站时，导游应与领队和行李员共同清点行李。

☆ 入住宾馆后，核对送达行李，并督促礼宾部及时将行李送至对应房间。

☆ 离店时，再次与领队和行李员共同清点行李，办理交接手续。

团队没有安排行李员的服务要点：

☆ 导游应提醒旅游者照看好自己的行李。

☆ 在交通港、离店等环节，提醒旅游者尤其注意，确认自己的行李装车。

063. What will you do when you find a tourist missing in the hotel before departure?（如在离店前发现少了一名旅游者，导游应如何处理？）

★ Wait for another 10-15 minutes and look for the tourist in all the places he/she might go to (such as a coffee shop, souvenir shop, cashier's desk, business center, bookstore, etc).

★ If you still fail to find him/her, call the office and leave a message for him/her at the hotel with your cell phone number. Arrange the group to leave for the port.

★ If there is still no news about the missing tourist before the group boards the plane/ship/train, call the office again. Report the case to the police if necessary.

★ Keep a record afterwards.

☆ 等候 10 ~ 15 分钟，在旅游者可能去的地方寻找，（如咖啡店、纪念品商店、外币兑换处、商务中心、书店等）。

☆ 如未找到，报告旅行社，在宾馆给旅游者留下写有地陪联系方式的便条。带领团队前往交通港。

☆ 如登机（船、火车）前，仍无消息，再次通知旅行社。必要时向公安机关报案。

☆ 做好相关记录留档。

【备注】《旅游法》第十六条规定：入境游客不得在境内非法滞留，随团入境的游客不得擅自分团、脱团。(According to Article 16 of *Tourism Law*: Inbound tourists are not allowed to stay within the territory of China illegally, or leave or separate from the group without permission if travelling in a group.)

《旅游法》第五十五条规定：旅游经营者组织、接待出入境旅游，发现游客从事违法活动或者有违反本法第十六条规定情形的，应当及时向公安机关、旅游主管部门或者我国驻外机构报告。(According to Article 55 of *Tourism Law*: When organizing and receiving inbound and outbound tourists, tourism operators shall timely report any illegal activity or circumstance that violates Article 16 of this law by the tourists to the public security organ, the tourism authority or Chinese institutions functioning abroad.)

遇到离港前旅游者迟到、未出现等情况，应当机立断，不可无原则地等待，以免造成更大的损失。

064. When should you arrive at the airport with a departing group? When should a group arrive at the railway station to await a departure?(旅游团应在飞机起飞前多长时间到达机场？应在火车出发前多长时间到达火车站？）

★ Three hours in advance of the scheduled departure time for international flights; two hours for domestic flights.

★ One hour before the train leaves.

☆ 国际航班应提前三小时到达机场；国内航班提前两小时。

☆ 乘火车应提前一小时到达火车站。

【备注】目前对此问题有不同的看法，如上海地区导游服务规范中规定：国际航班应提前2小时到达机场；国内航班提前1.5小时；乘火车需提前45分钟到达火车站。另外，一般在敏感时期，敏感城市或敏感事件发生后，安检时间会延长，导游送机前需关注相关信息，以便应对。

065. What are you supposed to do when you are seeing a group off at the airport?（在机场送团时，导游应做哪些工作？）

★ Double check the departure time and airline tickets.

★ Leave enough time to assist tourists to check in, locate the appropriate airline counter, check their locked luggage through to the next stop, get luggage claim tickets and boarding passes.

★ Walk tourists to the security check point and say goodbye to them.

☆ 再次确认出发时间和票据。
☆ 给旅游者留有足够时间办理行李托运，领取行李托运凭证和登机牌。
☆ 将旅游者带至安检处与之告别。

【备注】目前基本使用电子票据，导游需要提前电话确认票据（机票）。此外，导游需要特别注意接送站的具体地址。火车票一般是旅行社提前出好票交给导游，到站取票也可以，但比较费时。为防止遗失，导游一般在送站前发火车票给旅游者。高铁动车，可以用身份证直接上车，但外宾不可以，必须持票上车。

066. What should be included in a farewell speech?（欢送词应包括哪些部分？）

★ Have a quick review of the sightseeing activities.
★ Express your appreciation for their good cooperation and understanding.
★ Ask for advice on how guiding service can be improved.
★ Make an apology if there is room for improvement.
★ Hope that they will come back and you will be delighted to be their guide again and show them something new.

★ Wish them a pleasant journey.

☆ 简要回顾行程。
☆ 对旅游者的配合及理解表达谢意。
☆ 征求旅游者对接待工作的意见和建议。
☆ 如有不足之处，表达歉意。
☆ 希望旅游者再次光临并表达希望再次提供服务的愿望。
☆ 祝福旅游者旅行愉快。

067. Make a brief farewell speech.（致一个简短的欢送词。）

★ Good afternoon, ladies and gentlemen! Time goes quickly and your trip in Shanghai is drawing to a close. In the previous days we had a good time in many interesting places in Shanghai and in the city of Suzhou. Here I want to thank you for your cooperation and support. Also I shall apologize for any inconvenience in the trip due to various reasons. If you have any advice which may help us improve our service, please let me know. I hope next time when you are in Shanghai I will be your guide again. Wish you a pleasant trip back home.

☆ 女士们，先生们，下午好！时间过得很快，大家的上海之行就要结束了。在过去的几天里，我们愉快地游览了上海和苏州不少有趣的景点。在此，感谢大家的合作与支持。同时对旅途中因各种原因造成的不便，我表示歉意。如您对我们的服务有任何建议，请告诉我，以便我们改进。希望下次大家来上海的时候，我能再次成为大家的导游。祝大家旅途愉快。

【**备注**】以上是一篇最简单的欢送词，以涵盖欢送词各组成部分为标准。在实际工作中，一篇优秀的欢送词会给旅游者留下难忘的印象，因此导游要精心准备既涵盖基本要点又富有个人特点的欢送词。

068. What do you need to do after the group leaves?（旅游团离开后，导游还需做哪些工作？）

★ Finish the necessary paper work.

★ Settle accounts with the accounting department of the travel agency within the time limit; return items borrowed from the agency.

★ If there were any incidents that happened during the tour, like traffic accidents, missing passports, money stolen or passengers hospitalized, etc, submit a report and keep a record.

☆ 完成相关书面工作。

☆ 在规定时间内至旅行社财务部门办理相关手续，并归还所借旅行社的物品。

☆ 如在行程中发生诸如车祸、护照丢失、财物被窃、旅游者住院等事宜，导游需提交事件报告以备案。

Related words and phrases

baggage/luggage cart	行李手推车
trunk	大箱子
check-in suitcase	托运行李箱
shoulder bag	单肩包
backpack	双肩包
rolling carry-on case/bag	手提拉杆箱
flight schedule display	航班信息表
cancellation	取消
business class	商务舱
economy class	经济舱
connecting flight	转机
overweight	超重
excess luggage fee	超件行李费
baggage/luggage claim tag	行李认领牌
evaluation form	意见表（反馈表）

Questions for discussion

1. What is to be done before tourists leave for the airport at 6:00 in the morning?
2. What will you do when you are already at the airport with the group and are told that the plane is canceled due to bad weather?

Part Ⅱ The Tour Leader and the National Guide

领队和全陪服务流程与规范

听力音频

Unit 9 The Tour Leader 领队服务流程与规范

069. What is the tour leader?（何谓领队？领队的工作职责是什么？）

★ A tour leader (also referred to as the tour escort in Central America, or tour conductor in Japan) is assigned by the foreign travel service to accompany the tour group through the whole trip.

★ He/She accompanies the tour group throughout the trip, and makes sure that the local travel agency fulfills the contract obligations. He/She work together with the local guide and sometimes the national guide as well.

☆ 领队(在中美洲被称为“旅行陪同”,在日本被称为“观光领队”)是受海外旅行社委派，(代表该旅行社)带领旅游团从事旅游活动的工作人员。

☆ 领队全程陪同旅游者，从出发直至安全返回，确保地接社按照合同提供各项服务。领队与地陪，有时还有全陪，合作共事。

【备注】“领队”一词英文可用 tour leader，tour escort 和 tour lead，《旅游法》采用 tour lead 一词，业界普遍使用 tour leader，故本书采用业界常用表述 tour leader。

070. Basically there are five stages of outbound tour service. What are these stages?（出境领队服务主要有五个阶段，分别包括哪些？）

★ Preparation before departure.

★ Departure from China and entry into destination countries or regions.

★ Touring in destination countries or regions.

★ Departure from destination countries or regions and entry into China.

★ Follow-up work.

☆ 准备阶段。

☆ 中国出境与他国（地区）入境阶段。

☆ 境外旅游阶段。

☆ 他国（地区）离境及归国入境阶段。

☆ 后续工作。

071. What kind of preparations should the tour leader make before leaving for the destination country?（领队在带团出境前需要做的准备工作主要有哪些？）

★ Get to know the basic information of the group with the help of OP and get relevant documents.

★ Be familiar with the tourism reception plan.

★ Do a good job of verification.

★ Make a good preparation for items and knowledge needed.

★ Hold a Pre-departure briefing.

☆ 听取旅行社计调人员介绍团队情况和接受相关资料。

☆ 熟悉旅游接待计划。

☆ 做好查验核实工作。

☆ 做好物质与知识准备。

☆ 开好出境前说明会。

072. What kinds of information and documents should the tour leader get from the office?（听取旅行社计调人员介绍团队情况和接受相关资料时，导游应获取哪些信息和资料？）

★ Information of the group (including the composition of the tour group, key members, the itinerary, special arrangements and requirements, the arrangement for the pre-departure briefing).

★ Relevant documents mainly include: itinerary, Name List of Outbound Group of Chinese Citizens, entry and exit registration cards, customs declaration forms, travel documents, tourist visas/endorsements, transportation tickets, reception plans, address list, etc.

☆ 听取旅游计调人员介绍团队情况（主要包括旅游团构成情况、团内重点成员情况、团队旅游行程、该团特殊安排与要求、行前说明会的安排）。

☆ 接受计调人员移交有关资料，主要包括出境旅游行程表、《中国公民出国旅游团队名单表》、出入境登记卡、海关申报单、旅游证件、旅游签证/签注、交通票据、接待计划书、联络通讯录等资料。

【备注】《中国公民出国旅游团队名单表》一式四联，即出境边防检查专用联、入境边防检查专用联、旅游行政部门审核专用联和旅行社自留专用联。

073. What detailed information concerning tourism reception plan should the tour leader be familiar with?（关于旅游接待计划领队应熟悉哪些详细信息？）

★ Be familiar with the name of the travel company of the destination country (region); and get to know the contact person and his phone number.

★ Be familiar with the itinerary, such as time arrangement, means of transportation, all programs, hotels, entertainment and dining arrangements.

★ Be familiar with the members of the tour group, such as their names, gender, occupation, age, special members and special requirements.

☆ 熟悉目的地国家或地区接待社社名和联系方式。

☆ 熟悉旅游团行程计划，如旅游团抵离各地时间以及所乘交通工具、全部旅游项目、下榻饭店、文娱节目安排和用餐情况。

☆ 熟悉旅游团成员情况，如团员姓名、性别、职业、年龄段、特殊成员及特殊要求。

074. What details should the tour leader verify?(查验核实工作通常包括哪些细节？)

★ Check passports. Check the name, passport number, place of issue, date of issue, validity period, and signature.

★ Check visas. Carefully check the date of issue, the expiry date, and the visa number.

★ Check tickets. Whether it is a paper ticket or an e-ticket, the team leader needs to verify the passenger's name, date, flight number, and the airport if there is more than one airport in the city.

☆ 检查护照。重点检查姓名、护照号码、签发地、签发日期、有效期、有无本人签名等。

☆ 检查签证。领队应认真核实签发日期、截止日期、签证编号等。

☆ 检查机票。无论是纸质机票还是电子机票，领队需要核实乘机人姓名、乘机日期、航班号，如该城市有两个以上的机场，领队还需核实机场。

【备注】根据国际惯例，如果您需要前往其他国家，需要持有有效期半年以上的护照。目前，中国海关会核查申请人的护照，如果有效期不合格将有可能被拒绝出境。而目的地国家的海关，通常也会核查签证和护照有效期，不合格将有可能被拒绝入境。建议旅游者在出境前一定要关注自己的护照，有效期在6个月以上，如不足6个月请更换护照后再出行。

075. What kind of items and knowledge should the tour leader prepare?（物品与知识准备包括哪些？）

★ Make a good preparation for items needed. These mainly include: passports, air tickets and photocopies, airport tax and tour leader certificate, team fees, the tour flag, luggage tags, a couple of room allocation lists, self-adhesive labels for checked luggage, emergency phone numbers of destination countries, small gifts, Wi-Fi device and personal items, etc.

★ Make a good preparation for the basic information of the destination. Be familiar with the general picture of destination countries or regions, including history, geography, climate, national conditions, laws and regulations, customs and religious beliefs, taboos and customs clearance procedures, etc.

☆ 物品准备。主要包括：护照、机票及相关证件的复印件、机场税款和领队证、团队费用、社旗、行李标签、多份境外住房分配名单、托运行李所用不干胶标签、目的地国家报警或救助电话号码、小礼品、无线 Wi-Fi 设备及个人物品等。

☆ 知识准备。了解和熟悉目的地国家或地区基本情况，包括历史、地理、气候、国情、法律法规、风俗习惯和宗教信仰、禁忌，以及通关手续等。

076. What should the tour leader do in the pre-departure briefing?（在出境前说明会上，领队应做哪些工作？）

According to the time specified in the notice, the tour leader should hold a pre-departure briefing. The details are as follows:

★ Make a welcome speech: thank tourists for their trust in the travel agency and express desire to provide good services for tourists; wish them a smooth journey.

★ Distribute certain documents to tourists, mainly including the "travel product plan", itinerary, team logo, evaluation form of tourism service.

★ Tell tourists some precautions of outbound tourism, procedures of foreign currency exchange, etc.

★ Tell them the departure time and the meeting place and ask them to keep the telephone number of the tour leader.

按出团通知书约定的时间，召集旅游团成员举行“出境旅游行前说明会”。具体内容如下：

☆ 致欢迎词，包括感谢大家对旅行社的信任，表达为旅游者提供良好服务的愿望，预祝旅途顺利。

☆ 向旅游者发放资料，主要包括《旅游产品计划说明书》、出境旅游行程表、团队标识、旅游服务质量评价表。

☆ 说明出境旅游的有关注意事项以及外汇兑换事项与手续等。

☆ 说明旅游团出发时间和集合地点以及领队的联系方式。

077. Basically there are three stages before entering into the destination country or region. What are these stages?（在中国出境与他国入境阶段，领队服务主要分三个阶段，分别包括哪些？）

★ Departing from China.

★ In-flight service.

★ Entering the destination country (region).

☆ 中国出境阶段服务。

☆ 机上服务。

☆ 他国入境阶段服务。

078. What kind of services should the tour leader provide when the group is departing from China?（领队在中国出境阶段的工作流程主要包括哪些？）

★ Meet at the transportation port before departure.

★ Help tourists go through customs declaration procedures.

★ Assist in getting boarding cards and help with luggage check-in.

★ Go through health quarantine.

★ Go through the border inspection.

★ Go through the security check before boarding.

☆ 出发前出境口岸集合。

☆ 带领旅游者办理海关申报手续。

☆ 协助办理乘机及行李托运。

☆ 通过卫生检疫。

☆ 通过边防检查。

☆ 通过登机前的安全检查。

079. What kind of services can a tour leader provide for tourists when they are on the aircraft?（在飞行过程中，领队为旅游者提供的服务主要有哪些？）

★ Assist tourists to change seats if there are such requests.

★ Offer help at meal time and help communicate with flight attendant on special dining requirements.

★ Be familiar with the life-saving appliance and tell tourists how to use facilities on the aircraft.

★ Answer questions raised by tourists.

★ Help tourists fill in the entry form and customs declaration form.

☆ 协助旅游者调换座位（尽量不调换，或团内调换）。

☆ 用餐时为需要的客人提供（翻译）服务，关照特殊用餐要求。

☆ 熟悉飞机上的救生设备，指导机上设备使用。

☆ 解答旅游者提问。

☆ 帮助旅游者填写入境表和海关申报单。

080. What are the main procedures the group will go through when entering into the destination country or region?（他国入境阶段，领队的工作流程包括哪些？）

After the aircraft arrives at the airport of the destination country (region), a series of entry procedures must be handled. In different countries or regions, the sequence of procedures may be different.

★ Go through health quarantine.

★ Go through immigration formalities.

★ Claim checked luggage.

★ Go through customs clearance procedures.

★ Contact the local tour guide.

飞机抵达目的地国家（地区）的机场后，要办理一系列入关手续。各个国家（地区）对所需要办理的手续顺序并不完全一样。

☆ 经过卫生检疫。

☆ 办理入境手续。

☆ 领取托运行李。

☆ 办理入境海关手续。

☆ 与地接导游接洽。

081. What immigration formalities should the group go through?（办理入境手续主要包括哪些？）

★ After getting off the plane, the tour leader should lead the tourists to the immigration check-in counter to wait in front of any of the channels marked with foreigners' entry sign (FOREIGNER).

★ Provide the following documents to the immigration inspectors: passports, visas, tickets, and arrival cards. Sometimes immigration inspectors may ask tourists or the tour leader to present travel plans or hotel and airline ticket confirmations.

★ Go through the inquiry. The immigration inspector may make simple inquiries such as the reason for coming, the duration of stay, the number of group and so on. Tourists should respond calmly and honestly. After the inspector has verified the above information, he will stamp an entry stamp on the passport and give back the ticket and passport to tourists. Upon completion, tourists should courteously thank them.

☆ 下飞机后，领队应带领旅游者到入境检查柜台，在标有外国人入境（FOREIGNER）标识的任一通道前排队等候入关。

☆ 向入境检查人员交付入境所需的证件和文件：护照、签证、交通票据和入境卡。有的国家入境检查官会要求旅游者或领队出示旅游计划或入境酒店和机票确认单。

☆ 接受询问。入境检查官可能会就入境后的情况进行简单询问，如来此地原因、停留时间、同行人员和数量等；旅游者应如实而从容回答。入境官审核无误后，会在护照上加盖入境章，并将机票和护照退还旅游者。完毕，旅游者应礼貌致谢。

082. What procedures are included in customs inspection phase?（海关查验阶段主要包括哪些流程？）

★ Hand in customs declaration. The tour leader should help tourists hand in customs declaration forms, and tell tourists that they should be cooperative when they are asked to provide certain documents.

★ Be cooperative at random checks. Sometimes customs officials will ask tourists whether they have brought cigarettes and other restricted items and how many they have had. Tourists should answer questions honestly. In case tourists are asked to open their suitcases, they should be cooperative.

☆ 交付海关申报单。领队带领旅游者交付海关申报单，海关人员要求查验证件时要予以服从。

☆ 配合接受抽查。一般情况下，海关人员会口头询问旅游者是否带有香烟等物品、带了多少等问题，旅游者应如实回答。如遇被要求开箱检查，旅游者要予以配合。

083. What kind of services should the tour leader provide when the group is in the destination country or region?（旅游团在目的地国家或地区旅游时，领队应提供哪些服务？）

In the destination country or region, the tour leader should work with the local guide to fulfill the tourist contract. When providing service, the local tour guide usually plays a leading role while the tour leader offers assistance. In addition, the following work should also be done:

★ Consult with the local guide on the details of the travel schedule.
★ Make sure the local travel agencies fulfill the travel obligation.
★ Protect personal safety and property security of tourists.
★ Coordinate relationships and deal with conflicts if there are any.
★ Deal with emergencies.

旅游者在境外旅游期间，领队对旅游者服务须与地陪配合一起完成。提供服务时，须在以地陪为主、领队为辅的合作过程中进行。此外，领队还应做好如下工作：

☆ 商定旅游日程。
☆ 督促海外接待社履行旅游合同。
☆ 维护旅游者财产和生命安全。
☆ 协调关系，处理矛盾。
☆ 处理突发事件。

084. What are the principles the tour leader should follow when conducting a shopping tour?（在境外旅游的购物服务环节中，领队应遵循哪些原则？）

★ Make sure the shopping venues arranged by the local agency have a good reputation.

★ Make sure there is no pressure or misleading promotion from the tour leader when tourists are shopping.

★ Make sure the shopping tour is arranged according to the travel plan, and the local guide cannot increase shopping time or add shopping venues.

★ Ensure the local guide makes recommendation honestly.

★ Remind tourists to ask for formal invoices.

☆ 督促地接社安排信誉好的场所购物。

☆ 领队不引导、更不能误导旅游者购物。

☆ 领队应当制止地陪擅自增加购物次数和时间。

☆ 领队应当督促地陪如实介绍商品或服务。

☆ 提醒旅游者索要发票。

【备注】中国旅游者在境外的购买力有目共睹，但出境旅游购物被坑的事情也时有发生。境外退货比较复杂，因为很多商品都涉及退税环节，需要旅游者保存好商品的购物清单、退税单据等，需要先办理税金返还、然后退换货，再次退税。

085. What should the tour leader do to ensure safety of the tour group?（在境外旅游时，领队如何做好旅游团的安全保障工作？）

★ The tour leader should emphasize safety issues in the pre-departure briefing.

★ Frequently remind tourists to take good care of themselves and their belongings.

★ For different tourists and in different situations, the tour leader should give different, specific, and corresponding suggestions on safety.

★ Actions speak louder than words. The tour leader should mind his/her own behaviors and set a good example for group members.

☆ 领队必须认真开好行前说明会，并充分强调安全问题。

☆ 在旅游行程中进行警示和说明。

☆ 提醒和警示应当有针对性。

☆ 领队自身的行为必须合乎规范。

086. Basically there are three stages during departing from destination country (or region) and returning to China. What are these stages?（在他国出境与中国入境阶段，领队服务主要分三个阶段，分别包括哪些？）

★ Departing from the destination country (region).

★ In-flight service.

★ Returning to China.

☆ 他国出境服务。

☆ 机上服务。

☆ 中国入境阶段服务。

087. What services should the tour leader provide at the airport when departing from the destination country or region?（领队在机场协助办理他国出境的手续包括哪些？）

★ Help with check-in procedures.

★ Help with the departure procedure of immigration.

★ Help with customs formalities.

★ Help tourists claim tax refund.

★ Lead tourists to the boarding gate.

☆ 协助办理离境乘机手续。

☆ 协助办理移民局离境手续。

☆ 协助办理海关手续。

☆ 协助办理购物退税手续。

☆ 引领旅游者登机。

088. What services should the tour leader provide when arriving at the airport and before going through immigration formalities?(在到达机场、办理移民局离境手续前，领队应提供什么服务？)

★ Check in luggage.

★ Help tourists change boarding cards.

★ Distribute passports, boarding cards and luggage tickets.

★ Purchase airport tax if it is needed.

☆ 准备托运行李。

☆ 换领登机牌。

☆ 分发护照、登机牌和行李票。

☆（有需要的话）购买机场税。

【备注】通常情况下，国外机场收取的机场税会在购买机票时一并付清，但也有些国家的国际机场，机场税是不在机票中代收的，需要当场购买。

089. What are the departure formalities that the group will go through?（办理移民局离境手续包括哪些内容？）

★ Fill out the departure card.

★ Say goodbye to the local tour guide.

★ Go through the procedure for departure. Give the departure card, passport, the boarding card, etc. to the immigration officer for inspection. The inspector will stamp the passport with a departure stamp or a "USED" stamp on the visa. Then all items will be returned to tourists and the departure procedure is completed.

☆ 填写出境卡。

☆ 与地接导游道别。

☆ 依次办理离境手续。将出境卡、护照、登机牌等递给移民官，接受检查。查验无误，移民官会在护照上盖上离境印章或在签证盖过“已使用”(USED)的章，然后将所有物品交还旅游者，离境手续即告完成。

090. What kind of services should the tour guide provide when going through customs formalities?（在办理海关手续时，领队应提供哪些服务？）

★ Inform about and emphasize restrictions on items that can be carried. Since different countries have different restrictions on the items carried by passengers when they leave the country, the tour leader should inform tourists in advance to avoid unnecessary trouble.

★ Tell tourists that they should be cooperative when going through customs inspection.

☆ 告知并强调携带物品的限制。由于各国对旅客出境时所携带物品有不同的限制，领队应事先查询和了解，并告知旅游者，以便出境时申报。

☆ 告知旅游者配合接受海关检查。

091. What services can the tour leader offer when tourists claim tax refund at the airport?（旅游者在机场办理退税时，领队可提供哪些服务？）

★ Be familiar with tax refund procedure and regulations of the destination country (region), and inform tourists in advance.

★ Leave enough time for tax refund procedure due to the complexity of the claim process.

★ Inform tourists if items they bought have to be checked in, they should have officer stamp on the tax invoice.

★ If tourists fail to claim tax refund, the tour leader should tell tourists how they can claim refund in China.

☆ 不同国家退税税率和程序有所差别，领队应熟悉目的地国家（或地区）退税程序与规定，并告知旅游者。

☆ 因退税程序比较复杂，应留出足够的时间办理。

☆ 告知旅游者，如需要退税的物品必须托运，要先让票务人员在收据上盖章，方可退税。

☆ 如时间紧张，旅游者未来得及办理退税，可告知游客在国内办理退税的方式。

【备注】办退税耗时耗力，如果正值打折季或旅游旺季，排队的时间会很长。领队需计算好时间提前到达机场。欧洲有三个主要的退税公司，可选择不同的方式。只要退税单上印有“Alipay”手机号填写栏的标志，就意味着该商户支持退税到支付宝海外退税账户服务，可以通过支付宝办理退税。如时间紧张，可选择到国内办理，但须提醒旅游者到海关报税处盖章。并告知国内可退税的城市及银行等信息（可在退税公司网站上查询）。

092. What kind of services can the tour leader provide when leading tourists to the boarding gate?（引领旅游者登机阶段，领队应做好哪些工作？）

★ Check the boarding gate and boarding time. Sometimes the boarding gate and boarding time may change due to various reasons. Once it happens, make sure to inform tourists of the correct gate and updated boarding time.

★ Count the number of tourists. In order to prevent tourists from missing the plane due to hearty shopping or other reasons, the team leader should arrive at the boarding gate to count the number of guests in advance and contact the tourists who have not shown up.

☆ 核实登机闸口。领队应注意收听机场内广播，或向机场内的咨询台询问，或从电脑屏幕上查看所乘坐航班闸机口是否有改变；在确定无误后，要将正确的登机时间和闸口告诉旅游者。

☆ 清点人数。为避免旅游者因为购物等原因发生误机事件，领队应提前赶到登机闸口清点人数，与未能及时赶到的旅游者进行联系，确保准时登机。

093. What services should the tour leader provide when the group arrives at the Chinese airport?（归国入境阶段，领队应提供哪些服务？）

★ Go through formalities at the quarantine counter. The tour leader should lead tourists to the designated counter and submit the relevant card completed on the return flight. If everything goes well, the inspection and quarantine can be passed.

★ Go through border Inspection. The tour leader should lead tourists to the border check counter, and hand passports and boarding passes to the border inspectors one by one. After getting the stamp at the inspection counter, tourists can enter China.

★ Get checked luggage. Before leading tourists to the luggage carousel, make sure tourists have got their luggage tickets. Tourists should claim their own luggage and go through inspection. If some tourists fail to get their luggage, the leader should assist them handling the issue.

★ Go through customs inspection. The team leader should be familiar with the restrictions imposed by the Chinese Customs on the entry of items and inform tourists in advance. If a tourist needs to declare an item, a customs declaration form should be completed in advance. If there is nothing to declare, just skip this stage. When a tourist who has declared something for personal use when he leaves China, he is required to show his declaration form when he returns to China.

☆ 接受检验检疫。领队带领旅游者至柜台前，递交在返程飞机上填好的表格；如无意外，即可通过检验检疫。

☆ 接受入境边防检查。领队带领旅游者在边检柜台前排队，并逐一将护照和登机牌等交由边检人员查验，经其核准后在护照上加盖入境验讫章，并将护照还给旅游者，旅游者即可入境。

☆ 领取托运行李。领队在带领旅游者至行李转盘处之前，应将行李牌发给每位旅游者，由其各自认领自己行李，并交服务人员查验。若有旅游者行李遗失，领队应协助处理。

☆ 接受海关检查。领队应了解中国海关对入境物品的限制规定，并告知旅游者。如旅游者有需要申报的物品，应在入境飞机上填写海关申报单。如没有则无须填写。出境时旅游者经过申报的旅行自用物品，旅游者复带入境应出示出境时填写的申报单。

094. What should the tour leader do after the group finishes the tour?（团队结束行程后，领队需完成哪些后续工作？）

A complete outbound service begins with the handover of the schedule before the departure, and it ends when the tour leader hands over all documents and settles accounts. The follow-up work includes:

★ Carry out handover issue timely with the office and submit certain documents or records of some special cases. Documents that should be handed over mainly include "the tour leader's logbook", "the evaluation form of tour service", feedback of tourists, and summary of the tour, etc. If anything special and important happens during the tour, the tour leader should write a detailed report and submit it to the travel agency.

★ Settle accounts with accounting department timely. These include settling the accounts within the specified time; getting remuneration; return borrowed items to the office.

★ After the completion of service, it is highly suggested that the tour leader maintain a good relation with tourists. The tour leader can keep contact with tourists through various means. By doing this, the tour leader may win word of mouth and even repeat business for the agency.

领队一次完整的接团工作，是从团队出发前与旅行社计调的交接开始，到归来后与计调交接工作完成后结束。带团结束后续工作主要包括：

☆ 与组团社交接工作，交齐相关的书面资料，反馈特殊情况。领队应将相关的书面资料交给旅行社，其中包括《领队日志》《旅游服务质量评价表》、旅游者书面意见以及接团工作小结等。如带团期间遭遇特殊问题或重要情况，领队都应以书面报告的形式进行详细记录，并交旅行社保存。

☆ 账务处理工作。按照旅行社要求按时进行报账；领取带团酬劳；归还所借物品。

☆ 接团结束后，与旅游者保持良好联系。旅游结束后，领队还可通过多种方式与旅游者保持情感联系，使旅游者对领队以及旅行社留下良好印象，为旅行社争取回头客。

Related words and phrases

domestic tourism	境内旅游
outbound tourism	出境旅游
border tourism	边境旅游
inbound tourism	入境旅游
mass tourism	大众旅游
refund	退款
service charge/commission	手续费
over-weight luggage	超重行李

luggage claim area	行李认领区
declaration	申报
invoice	发票
Duty-free stores	免税店
Tax refund	退税

Questions for discussion

1. During the process of flight check-in, a tourist is found to have luggage overweight. How will you help the tourist?
2. One of your tourists will be late for the flight check-in for 30 minutes. What will you do to help him?

听力音频

Unit 10 The National Guide 全陪服务流程与规范

095. What is the national guide? What are the two categories of national guides? With whom do they cooperate when providing services?（何谓全陪？全陪分为哪两种？他们的合作对象分别是谁？）

A national guide, also known as a tour director or tour manager, is someone who leads a group throughout a country or part of a country. He/She supervises and assists the local travel agency, local guides, and related service providers to ensure that the travel plan of the organizing travel agency is implemented as agreed.

There are two kinds of national guides: the national guide for inbound group and the national guide for domestic group.

The national guide for inbound group works with the tour leader and the local guide, forming the serving team.

The domestic national guide cooperates with the local guide of each stop, forming the serving team.

全陪是监督并协助地接社、地陪及相关接待者的服务，以使组团社的旅游接待计划得以按约实施，为旅游者提供境内全程陪同导游服务的人员。

全陪分为入境旅游团全陪和国内旅游团全陪。

入境旅游团全陪与境外领队、地陪共同组成导游服务集体。

国内旅游团全陪与地陪共同组成导游服务集体。

096. Basically there are six stages in terms of working procedures of the national guide. What are these stages?（全陪服务主要分六个阶段，分别包括哪些？）

★ Preparation.

★ Meeting the group (at the airport) in the first stop.

★ Helping the local guide in each city.

★ Providing service when the group is moving to the next stop.

★ Departure service.

★ Dealing with unsettled matters if there are any.

☆ 服务准备工作。

☆ 首站迎接服务。

☆ 协助各站导游服务。

☆ 途中服务。

☆ 末站（离境站）送团服务。

☆ 后续工作。

097. What kind of preparations should the national guide make before picking up the group?（全陪在接团前需要做的准备工作主要有哪些？）

★ Be familiar with details of the tourism reception plan.

★ Make a good preparation for items needed and related knowledge.

★ Psychological preparation is also essential.

☆ 熟悉旅游接待计划。

☆ 做好物质与知识准备。

☆ 做好心理准备。

098. What should the national guide do when meeting the group at the first stop?（在首站接团阶段，全陪应做好哪些工作？）

★ Checking with the local travel agency on details of picking-up.

★ Picking up the overseas tour group or meeting the domestic group.

★ Giving the first tour presentation to the group (usually a welcome speech and an introduction to China).

★ Checking and talking over the schedule with the local guide.

☆ 同地接社核实接站事宜。

☆ 境外旅行团接站或境内旅行团集合。

☆ 首次讲解。

☆ 与地陪商谈日程。

099. What should the national guide do when the group is moving from a city to another?（旅游团在目的地城市转移途中，全陪应提供什么服务？）

★ Always give priority to tourists' safety.

★ Maintain a cheerful atmosphere.

★ Give presentations on some topics in which tourists are interested and answer questions.

★ Take care of tourists and offer timely help.

☆ 保障旅游者的安全。

☆ 保持欢快的气氛。

☆ 讲解与解答问题。

☆ 照顾好旅游者，及时提供帮助。

100. On what occasions does the national guide need to give tour presentation?（全陪在哪几种场合需要承担讲解任务？）

★ After meeting the group at the airport, the national guide needs to give a welcome speech, a brief introduction to the itinerary and dos and don'ts in the country.

★ When the group is moving from one city to another, the national guide is expected to give presentations en route.

★ Give a summary of the whole trip before the group is leaving Chinese mainland.

★ Sometimes the national guide will act as the local guide, giving tour presentations to destinations.

☆ 旅游团入境后全陪需要致欢迎词、介绍行程和提醒注意事项。

☆ 旅游团从甲城市到乙城市的途中，全陪需要做沿途讲解。

☆ 旅游团离境前，全陪应该对整个旅程做总结性发言。

☆ 全陪有时需要兼任地陪工作，担当目的地的讲解任务。

101. What service should the national guide provide when the national guide is to see the group off at the last stop?（末站送团阶段，全陪应做好哪些工作？）

★ Double check details of departure a day before the departure day.

★ Help with some unsettled issues if there are any.

★ Try to do some promotion to win repeat business.

★ Make a farewell speech.

★ See the group off at the airport.

☆ 提前一天落实有关送站事宜。

☆ 协助旅游者处理出境前的有关事务。

☆ 做好回头客营销工作。

☆ 致欢送词。

☆ 送别、协助旅游团离境/离开。

102. What services should a national guide provide when seeing the group off at the airport?（在机场送别、协助旅游团离境/离开过程中，全陪应提供哪些服务？）

★ Arrive at the airport at least 3 hours in advance for the inbound tour group (2 hours in advance for the domestic group).

★ Remind tourists to take good care of luggage and remind tourists not to put passports (ID Cards for domestic tourists) in checked luggage.

★ If inbound tourists buy something special such as cultural relics or Chinese medicine, tell them to carry the invoices and other documents with them.

★ Tell the tour leader and tourists how to go through certain formalities.

★ Bid farewell to tourists.

☆ 出境旅游团至少提前 3 小时到达机场（国内航班提前 2 小时）。

☆ 敦促旅游者带好行李物品，提醒旅游者出境时带好护照（国内旅游者带好身份证），切勿把护照（身份证）放入托运行李。

☆ 如购买文物或贵重药材等特殊商品，提醒旅游者将发票等有关证明准备好。

☆ 向领队与旅游者介绍办理出境手续的有关规定。

☆ 再次向旅游者道别。

103. What issues are included in the follow-up stage?（全陪在后续阶段应完成哪些工作？）

★ Handle the issues unsettled.

★ Fill in the "the national guide's logbook".

★ Settle the account within the time required.

★ Report to the office orally problems and emergencies happened during the tour.

★ Submit reports on important issues.

☆ 处理旅游团遗留问题。

☆ 填写《全陪日志》。

☆ 在规定时间去财务部门结清账目。

☆ 以口头形式汇报在旅游过程中发生的问题。

☆ 重大问题写出书面报告。

Related words and phrases

carrying capacity	承载能力
corporate image	公司形象
itinerary/schedule	团队行程
program	日程安排
identifying cardboard/sign board	标志牌
loudspeaker	喇叭
tour guide qualification certificate	导游资格证
guiding license/tour guide certificate	导游证
window seat	靠窗户的座位
aisle seat	靠过道的座位
economy (1-star)	一星级（酒店）
some comfort (2-star)	二星级（酒店）
average comfort (3-star)	三星级（酒店）
high comfort (4-star)	四星级（酒店）
luxury (5-star)	五星级（酒店）

Questions for discussion

1. What should the national guide do if 3 reserved double rooms are not available, instead, tourists are given 2 triple rooms，but they find this unacceptable?
2. What will you do if a tourist complains to you that the local guide is rather rude when the tourist refuse to buy things in the designated shop?

Part Ⅲ Special Care for Special Groups

特殊旅游群体服务

听力音频

Unit 11 FIT 散客服务

104. What are the reasons for the rapid development of FIT tourism?（散客旅游迅速发展的原因有哪些？）

★ People have more disposable money so they have more choices when making travel plans.

★ Tourists are becoming more and more experienced.

★ Transportation is more convenient.

★ With the increasing popularity of internet, tourists have more information sources so they can arrange almost everything by themselves before departure.

★ Reception conditions in many destinations are greatly improved, therefore tourists do not need to worry about services.

☆ 人们可支配收入增加，因此在制订旅游计划时选择更多。

☆ 旅游者经验日渐丰富。

☆ 交通越来越便捷。

☆ 随着网络的普及，旅游者制订外出旅游计划时信息渠道丰富，旅游者可以提前安排旅游各环节。

☆ 旅游目的地的接待条件日益改善，旅游者无须担心服务环节。

105. What are the characteristics of FIT?（散客有哪些特点？）

★ Less people (no more than 9 tourists).

★ More batches of reservation.

★ Shorter reservation time.

★ More individual requests.

★ More flexible itinerary and more changes.

☆ 批量小（不超过 9 人）。

☆ 批次多。

☆ 预订期短。

☆ 要求多。

☆ 变化多。

【备注】FIT 原为 foreign individual/independent tourist/ tour 的缩写，意为“去异地独立旅游（者）”现在更多地指 flexible independent travel。散客并不意味着全部旅游事务都由旅游者自己办理，实际上不少散客旅游活动都借助旅行社的帮助，如机票、旅馆等。因散客旅游灵活、自由，可选择性强，因此被越来越多的旅游者所青睐。国内散客也渐成旅游业主体。统计显示，近年来我国旅游市场每年都在高速增长，其中散客旅游人数增长最为明显，每年增长达 30%，而传统组团游增长速度只有 15%，且有增速放缓的趋势。因而，导游员要了解散客的特点及服务技能。

106. What are the difference between package tour and FIT tour?（散客旅游与团队旅游的区别是什么？）

★ For package tour, the itinerary is arranged by travel agency; for FIT tour, the itinerary is decided by tourists.

★ Different scales: There are at least 10 tourists in a package tour while an FIT tour contains no more than 9 tourists.

★ Different content: Package tour is carried out according to the tourist contract while FIT tour is more flexible in choosing programs.

★ Different ways of payment: For package tour, travel expenses are paid before the tour starts while for FIT, expenses are usually paid on the spot.

★ Different prices: Generally speaking, FIT enjoys fewer discounts so it is more expensive.

★ FIT tour is more challenging for the tour guide because there is no national guide or tour leader.

☆ 旅游方式不同：旅游团队行程由旅行社安排，散客的行程则是自行安排。

☆ 人数不同：旅游团队一般是 10 人及以上，散客则是

9人及以下。

☆ 服务内容不同：团队服务内容丰富且按计划进行，散客旅游服务项目通常较少且随意性较强。

☆ 付款方式不同：团队旅游费用在出游前一次性支付，散客旅游则是零星现付。

☆ 价格不同：通常散客的费用折扣较少，因而较贵。

☆ 服务难度不同：散客旅游没有领队和全陪，服务难度更大。

107. What are the characteristics of FIT service?（散客导游服务的特点有哪些？）

★ Less programs. Some FIT service only contains picking-up and hotel arrangement.

★ Shorter time.

★ More complicated. (This is due to the following facts: Firstly, there is no national guide and tour leader; secondly, tourists are of different background and even different nationalities; thirdly, the tour guide has little time getting familiar with tourists.)

★ More flexible service. (FITs are more independent and they have more requirements and changes.)

☆ 服务项目少，有些只包含接站和安排酒店。

☆ 服务周期短。

☆ 服务相对复杂（主要原因是没有领队或全陪、旅游者背景丰富、导游与旅游者不熟悉）。

☆ 服务更加灵活机动（散客自主意识强、服务要求多、变化多）。

108. How to do a good job in picking up FIT?（如何做好散客的接站工作？）

★ Get well-prepared for picking up tourists.

★ Arrive at the airport 30 minutes in advance.

★ Wait at the arrival gate for 20 minutes after the plane lands. (It won't take long for customs formalities and immigration procedures. If the tour guide is not there when the tourists show up, the guide might miss them.)

☆ 接站前做好充分准备。

☆ 提前 30 分钟到达机场。

☆ 飞机落地 20 分钟内，导游不要离开现场。（旅游者一般过海关和边检都很快。如果旅游者出来时没找到接站的导游，有可能会与导游擦肩而过。）

109. What can be the possibilities if you fail to see the tourists show up at the arrival gate after waiting for a long time and how to deal with the problem?（一般没有按时接到旅游者会出现哪几种可能？如何应对？）

<u>A. Tourists miss your welcome sign board and pass by...（旅游</u>

者没有看到你的接站牌……）

★ Stand at an unobstructed place at the arrival gate to make sure that everybody can notice your sign board before he/she passes by.

★ Look for those whose number (maybe a couple or maybe a family of 4), gender or age are in accordance with that of yours on the assignment sheet and keep an eye on those whose attire might suggest a little bit of nationality if there is any.

★ Don't hesitate to go over and check with those targeted people and make sure that they are not your clients before they pass by.

☆ 站在出口醒目地点，高举写有旅游者名字的接站牌，尽量使所有出来的人都能看到。

☆ 仔细捕捉那些符合你接待人数（或许是一对夫妇，也可能是一家四口）、性别、年龄及带有客源国旅游者穿着打扮特点的旅游者。

☆ 不厌其烦上前询问。

B. Tourists are met by their friends or go with someone else who was on the same flight...（旅游者被他的朋友接走了或是跟着同机熟人走了……）

★ Call the hotel and leave a message for tourists with your cell phone number, so they can contact you upon their arrival at the hotel.

☆ 打电话给宾馆并给旅游者留言，让旅游者一抵达宾馆就与你联系。

C. Tourists see the hotel welcome sign first and go with the hotel representative stationed at the airport...（客人被酒店驻机场代表接走了……）

★ Before the plane lands, check with the hotel representative stationed at the airport to see whether he/she also has a list with the same tourists to be picked up. If affirmative, let him/her know that you are from a local travel agency to meet these tourists. If he/she meets them first, ask him/her to inform you.

☆ 航班抵达前，向宾馆驻机场代表查询，他们是否也有相同旅游者的接站名单。如有，告诉他/她，你是旅行社派来接旅游者的，如他/她先看到旅游者，请他/她及时通知你。

D. Tourists find luggage missing and stay with the airline representative to deal with the problem...（旅游者没有拿到行李，还在与航空公司交涉……）

★ Wait longer or ask for help from the airport staff to see if your tourists are at the luggage claim counter.

☆ 再多等一点时间，或让机场工作人员帮你查找你的旅游者是否在行李查询处。

E. Tourists miss the flight from the last stop...（旅游者没

有赶上飞机……）

★ Call the office and wait for further instructions. If there is another plane from the same airline and same airport coming soon, wait for the next flight.

☆ 报告办公室，等候指示。如有同一航空公司从同一机场起飞的下一航班，间隔时间又不是很长的，可以继续等待。

110. What kind of services can you offer for FIT tourists when they are checking in at the hotel? （在散客入住酒店服务环节，导游可提供哪些服务？）

★ Help with check-in procedures.

★ Confirm the schedule if there are any.

★ Confirm details of the delivery service.

★ Try to promote some programs in a smart way.

☆ 帮助办理酒店入住手续。

☆ 确认日程安排。

☆ 确认送机服务细节。

☆ 灵活推销旅游项目。

111. What are you supposed to do before you say good-bye to tourists and leave the hotel? （在离开酒店和散客告别前，导游还应做哪些工作？）

★ Double check the departure time and place.

★ Get an up-to-date rooming list from the front desk.

★ Leave behind your mobile phone number for further contact.

★ Tell tourists that you will inform them the day before departure about luggage collection, the meeting point and departure time.

★ If you are not the same guide who will send tourists off, provide the next guide with all the necessary information of the tourists through office. Let the tourists know whom to expect and how to contact him/her.

☆ 核对旅游者离开本站时的时间和交通港。

☆ 向总台索要旅游者房单。

☆ 留下自己的联系方式，如手机号码。

☆ 告知旅游者离开本站前一天晚上，你会联系他们，商定次日行李运送方式、集合地点和接客时间。

☆ 若不是你送客，应及时把旅游者的一切信息通过办公室转告下一位陪同。告诉旅游者下一位陪同的联系方式。

112. What kind of services can you offer for VIP FIT tourists during sightseeing?（重点散客游览服务要点有哪些？）

★ Tour guides should communicate with tourists in advance, giving suggestions on arrangements. Let tourists make the final decision.

★ Conduct the tour at a moderate speed.

★ Interaction is important. In addition to the necessary introduction, tour guides may conduct the tour in the form of dialogue or discussion.

★ Answer questions timely and satisfy their reasonable requests if possible.

★ Conduct the tour according to the contract. Do not compress or extend the agreed time.

☆ 对于游览路线，导游要积极与旅游者沟通，给出建议，由旅游者决定。

☆ 控制好速度，劳逸结合。

☆ 讲解时注意互动，除了必要的介绍外，可采用对话或讨论的形式进行讲解。

☆ 对于旅游者的问题和合理诉求，尽量现场回答或满足。

☆ 控制游览时间，不可随意压缩或延长约定时间。

113. When an FIT asks you to take him to pornographic venues, what will you do?（当客人提出要求去不健康的娱乐场所时，导游应如何应对？）

★ The guide should explain patiently and refuse his request.

★ Introduce Chinese traditional ideas and moral standards.

★ Tell the tourist that going to such places is illegal in China. Therefore, the guide will not arrange the tourist to visit or take part in projects or activities that violate the Chinese laws, legal provisions and social morals.

☆ 导游应耐心解释并拒绝该要求。
☆ 介绍中国的传统观念和道德标准。
☆ 指出去不健康的娱乐场所在中国是违法的。所以导游不会为旅游者安排参观或者参与违反我国法律、法规和社会公德的项目或者活动。

【备注】导游在处理类似问题时，应考虑到文化差异，注意方式方法。根据《旅游法》第四十一条规定：导游和领队从事业务活动，应当佩戴导游证、领队证，遵守职业道德，尊重旅游者的风俗习惯和宗教信仰，应当向旅游者告知和解释旅游文明行为规范，引导旅游者健康、文明旅游，劝阻旅游者违反社会公德的行为。(According to Article 41 of *Tourism Law*: When providing services, tour guides/tour leads shall wear their tour guide certificate/tour lead certificate, observe professional ethics, respect the custom and religious beliefs of tourists, tell and explain to the tourists norms of civilized tourist behaviors, guide the tourists to travel in a healthy and civilized way, and stop behaviors which violate social morality.)

114. What will you do if you fail to find the FIT who is due to check out and leave for the airport?（导游到达散客下榻的酒店后，没找到要送站的散客，该如何应对？）

★ Try to contact the tourist. If the tourist cannot be reached, the tour guide should do the following things.

★ Check with the front desk whether the tourist has left.

★ Together with the driver, look for the tourists for 20 minutes.

★ If the tour guide fails to find the tourist, report to the office for assistance.

★ If all efforts are in vain, leave the hotel after getting the instruction of the office.

☆ 联系该客人，如客人无法联络，则按以下步骤行事。

☆ 到饭店前台了解客人是否已离店。

☆ 与司机共同寻找约 20 分钟。

☆ 向办公室报告并请求协助查询。

☆ 确认无法找到客人，经旅行社同意后，导游方可离开宾馆。

Related words and phrases

pick-up and delivery service	接送服务
shuttle bus	班车/摆渡车
limousine	豪华轿车

MPV/Multi-Purpose Vehicle	商务车
SUV/Sports Utility Vehicle	越野车
laundry service	洗衣服务
ethnic food	民族风味餐
specialty restaurant (local flavor restaurant)	风味餐厅
force majeure/events unavoidable	不可抗力
terminate the contract	终止合同
additional fees hence incurred	由此产生的额外费用

Questions for discussion

1. What will you do when an FIT tells you that he/she wants to buy some knockoff（名牌仿制品） Gucci handbags?
2. What will you do when an FIT insists you bargaining in a shopping plaza?

听力音频

Unit 12 Special Groups 特殊群体服务

115. What kind of services will you provide for elderly tourists?（如何做好老年旅游者的服务工作？）

★ Speak clearly at suitable speed and make yourself heard and understood.

★ When you conduct a tour, walk at a moderate pace.

★ Emphasize important information and once in a while give them a friendly reminder to take care of their valuables, watch their steps and be aware of their surroundings in tourist spots.

★ Be patient with their questions.

★ Always care about the health and safety of tourists. Assist tourists getting on and off the coach. When offering a helping hand, give enough consideration to maintaining their dignity.

★ Be thoughtful and solve problems in a smart way.

☆ 说话时应发音清晰，语速适宜，使旅游者能听见听懂。

☆ 控制旅游行程节奏，控制行走速度。

☆ 重要信息反复强调；经常友情提示老年旅游者保管好贵重物品，注意脚下安全，在景点注意周边环境。

☆ 耐心回答老年旅游者的问题。

☆ 关注旅游者的健康安全，协助他们上下车。在提供帮助时，注意方式方法，以维护旅游者尊严。

☆ 善解人意，遇事灵活解决。

【备注】老年旅游者服务，可总结为“慢、耐心、细心”。其中“慢”包含两个方面：语速和行进速度；“耐心”体现在信息重复、友情提醒、回答问题；“细心”则要求提供必要的帮助及注意帮助的方式方法。《旅行社老年旅游服务规范》（以下简称《规范》）行业标准已由国家旅游局批准并予以公布，自2016年9月1日起实施。《规范》明确：老年游客指年龄在60周岁以上（含60周岁）的老年旅游产品的消费者。尤其值得关注的是，《规范》规定：包机、包船、旅游专列和100人以上的老年旅游团应配备随团医生服务。

116. What kind of services will you provide for a religious group?（如何接待宗教旅游团？）

★ Keep in mind religious policy stipulated in our constitution.

★ Try to get basic information about your tourists including their religion, sect and practices before you meet the group.

★ Avoid discussing religious matters. Don’t make any comments on religions; never compare different religious beliefs.

★ Respect different religions and religious practice. Pay attention to details and offer help for their religious practice when necessary.

★ Upon request, share China's religious policy with them.

☆ 熟记我国宪法规定的宗教政策。

☆ 接团前了解旅游者宗教信仰基本情况，如何种宗教、宗教派别及宗教活动。

☆ 不与旅游者讨论宗教事宜。不对任何宗教发表评论，尤其不在旅游者面前对不同宗教信仰进行比较。

☆ 尊重旅游者宗教信仰及习惯。注意服务细节，必要时为旅游者宗教活动提供方便。

☆ 如旅游者要求，可向其介绍中国宗教政策。

【备注】《旅游法》第十条规定：旅游者的人格尊严、民族风俗习惯和宗教信仰应当得到尊重 (According to Article 10 of *Tourism Law*: The human dignity, national customs and religious beliefs of tourists shall be respected.)。针对有宗教信仰的旅游者的导游服务，可总结为“知己知彼，少说多做”。“知己知彼”指了解中国宗教政策及旅游者的宗教信仰情况；“少说”指少讨论、少评论、少比较，“多做”指多注意服务细节，提供必要方便。

117. What kind of services will you provide for those who come for conventions?（如何为会展旅游团提供服务？）

★ Get basic information about the convention.

★ Offer warm and helpful service to the participants and staffs. Provide necessary information including airport pick-up/sent-off and hotel registration.

★ Do a good job as an interpreter or assistant at the information desk.

★ Offer a good sightseeing tour before or after the convention upon request.

☆ 接团前了解会展基本信息。

☆ 为参展者及其人员提供周到的服务，包括机场接送、酒店入住登记和提供必要的信息。

☆ 如问询台的翻译或工作人员那样做好信息咨询服务。

☆ 应旅游者要求，安排好会前和会后的观光旅游。

【备注】会展/会议旅游由于其兼容性强、辐射面广、层次高等特点，迅速成为一种新兴的旅游业态。英文中“会展旅游”的表述较多，如 business tour/trip, convention tour, conference tour, meeting tour 等。通常参会者会选择在会后进行游览，即“会后旅游”，英文可用“post-meeting tour”，“post-convention excursion”，或“post-conference trip”表示。

118. What special attention should a tour guide pay to children tourists?（带团过程中，如何做好儿童旅游者的服务工作？）

The tour guide should do the following things:

★ He/She may help take care of children tourists (for example, if the guide is not busy, he/she may tell stories to children tourists).

★ The guide should remind parents to take good care of children from time to time.

★ If children are sick, the guide should suggest parents send children to hospital immediately.

★ While helping take care of children tourists, the guide should keep in mind that his/her obligation is to provide service for the whole group.

The tour guide should not do the following things:

★ The guide should not take children alone with him/her when touring.

★ The guide should not buy food or toys for children.

★ When children are not comfortable, the guide should not offer any medicine or give suggestions on medicine.

★ The guide should not neglect cultural differences. For example, if tourists are from countries like Thailand, the guide should not praise their children for their appearance, nor should he/ she touch the heads of children.

导游应做以下事情：

☆ 可帮助照顾孩子（比如，有空时导游可讲故事给孩子听）。

☆ 行程中时常提醒家长照顾好孩子。

☆ 如孩子生病，应建议家长及时送其诊治。

☆ 在照顾好儿童的同时，导游一定要服务好其他旅游者。

导游要避免去做以下事情：

☆ 游览中，导游不要单独领着孩子。

☆ 不应给孩子买玩具与食品。

☆ 孩子不舒服时，导游不给孩子服药或建议其服什么药。

☆ 导游不要忽视文化差异。比如，在与泰国旅游者交往时，不要赞美其婴儿漂亮，也不要抚摸孩子的头。

【备注】为方便记忆，接待儿童旅游者要点可归纳为“四要”和“四不要”。跟儿童相关的团型一般包括亲子团和研学团，这两个团型的接待都要求安全第一，且导游应选择符合儿童认知规律的服务讲解方式。

119. What are the characteristics of the professional delegation? How will you conduct the tour?（考察旅游团具有哪些特征？导游如何带此类团？）

Characteristics of the professional delegation include the following aspects:

★ They have professional knowledge in certain aspect;

their purposes are clear; they observe carefully and have more professional questions; they have high expectation to tour presentation.

When providing services, the tour guide should pay attention to the following aspects:

★ The tour guide should make good knowledge preparation for the group.

★ When giving the tour presentation, the tour guide may play to his/her strengths. (For example, he/she may explain from an appropriate perspective).

★ Make sure tourists have enough time for further exploration by themselves.

专业考察团的特点包括：

☆ 旅游者通常专业知识丰富、目的明确、观察细致、专业问题多，对讲解要求高。

提供服务时，应注意以下几点：

☆ 导游事前的知识准备要充分。

☆ 讲解时要扬长避短（如积极寻找合适的讲解切入点）。

☆ 给旅游者留下足够的自由探索时间。

【备注】不同的考察旅游团目的和兴趣点不同，导游前期的知识准备格外重要；讲解时可避开专业知识性介绍，多结合当地情况，收集相关历史及风土人情等。如是政府考察团，则须格外注意讲解的准确性和精炼性，同时严守保密要求。

120. What kind of services should a guide provide for the adventure tour group?（导游应如何为探险旅游团提供服务？）

★ The guide himself/herself should be strong enough and has professional knowledge.

★ The guide should make adequate preparation and remind tourists to make preparation for the adventure tour.

★ The guide should be thoughtful and careful when conducting the tour.

★ When dealing with problems, the guide should be decisive and determined.

☆ 导游本人应具备强壮的身体和专业知识。

☆ 做好并提醒旅游者做好充分的探险准备。

☆ 导游服务周到、细心。

☆ 处理问题要果断。

【备注】《旅游法》第四十七条规定：经营高空、高速、水上、潜水、探险等高风险旅游项目，应当按照国家有关规定取得经营许可。此外，对于高风险旅游项目，旅行社还应提示并建议旅游者投保人身意外伤害保险。《旅游法》第六十一条规定：旅行社应当提示参加团队旅游的旅游者按照规定投保人身意外伤害保险。(According to Article 47 of *Tourism Law*: In order to engage in the operation of high-risk tourism projects like those conducted high up in the sky, at a high speed, or on the water, diving, adventure, etc., one shall first obtain a business license in accordance with relevant regulations of the State. According to Article 61: The travel agency shall remind the tourists in a tourism group of purchasing insurance against accidental death or any unexpected injury.)

121. What are the general psychological characteristics of disabled tourists? And what kind of services will you provide for them?（残障旅游者普遍的心理特征有哪些？对此导游应提供怎样的服务？）

Many disabled tourists are very sensitive, with sense of inferiority and loneliness, while most of them are full of compassion.

When providing services, the tour guide should pay attention to the following aspects:

★ Provide special service according to different cases.

★ Offer a helping hand when getting on and off the coach.

★ Conduct the tour at a moderate pace.

★ When offering a helping hand, give enough consideration to maintaining their dignity.

★ Be thoughtful and solve problems in a smart way.

不少残障旅游者非常敏感，有一定的自卑感、孤独感，却常常富有同情心。

提供服务时应注意以下几点：

☆ 根据残障人士的身体情况，做好针对性接待。

☆ 在上下车时适时提供帮助。

☆ 控制游览速度。
☆ 在提供帮助时，注意方式方法，以维护旅游者的尊严。
☆ 善解人意，遇事灵活解决。

【备注】要对残障旅游者给予必要的照顾，但要注意场合和分寸，当众过多的照顾有可能伤及他们的自尊心，适得其反。为做好有针对性的接待，可注意如下方面：对视力障碍者，导游讲解时应更加形象，能用手触摸的，让他们摸一摸，能聆听的，让他们安静地听一听；对于听力障碍者，不管是在车上还是在游览中，尽量将他们安排在靠前的位置；对于行动不便的旅游者，制订计划时要考虑是否需要轮椅，并提前通知相关部门做好准备，车辆也要选择方便轮椅上下的车，景点和饭店应有"无障碍设计"。另外，《旅游法》第十一条规定：残疾人、老年人、未成年人等旅游者在旅游活动中依照法律、法规和有关规定享受便利和优惠(According to Article 11 of *Tourism Law*: The disabled, the elderly and the minors shall enjoy due convenience and benefits in tourism activities in accordance with laws, regulations and relevant rules.)。

122. What are the characteristics of business group? What kind of services will you provide for a business group?（商务旅游团的特点是什么？导游应为此类商务团提供怎样的服务？）

Business travelers set clear goals for their travel. They are efficient and less price-sensitive, with higher expectation to service.

When providing services, the tour guide should pay attention to the following aspects:

★ Make sure the hotel is well-equipped, with necessary office facilities.

★ The tour guide and other staff should be punctual and efficient.

★ The tour guide should maintain a good professional image and know common business etiquette.

商务旅游者目标明确，讲求效率，对价格不敏感，对服务水平要求高。服务要点如下：

☆ 酒店应设施良好，具备办公设施。

☆ 导游及其他相关服务人员工作应守时且高效。

☆ 导游应注意个人形象并掌握常用的商务礼仪。

【备注】酒店的选择是旅行社计调在制订接待计划时所考虑的，非导游所能决定。但导游可将相关酒店的情况反馈给计调，以便计调在后续接待计划制订时有更好的选择和安排。

Related words and phrases

incentive tour	奖励旅游
cruise service	邮轮旅游
business travel	商务旅游
package tour	包价旅游

special interest tour	专门兴趣旅游
venue	会场，场地
the main hall	大厅
private room	包厢
annual meeting	年会
registration form	登记表
high-risk tourism project	高风险旅游项目
a business license	经营许可

Questions for discussion

1. How will you provide good service for pupils aged 7 to 8?
2. Your next group is a special one which is called "JEWISH HERITAGE OF SHANGHAI". What will you do to guarantee good service of this group?

Part Ⅳ Dealing with Individual Requests and Handling Emergencies and Common Issues

导游应变能力

听力音频

Unit 13 Dealing with Individual Requests 旅游者个别要求处理

123. How should a tour guide deal with individual requests?（导游应如何处理旅游者的个别诉求？）

A group consists of many people of various backgrounds. There will be individual requests in different situations from different tourists. When facing this, a tour guide shall follow the basic rules:

★ Firstly listen to the tourists carefully. (It is very important to show tourists that you really pay attention to what they request. You can't simply reject tourists even if the request is not reasonable. Your rejection may make them think you don't care for them.)

★ Figure out whether the request is reasonable and feasible. (You may consult with the tour leader or the national guide as they accompany the tourists all the time and they know them more than you do.)

★ If the request is both reasonable and feasible, report it to the travel agency and try to arrange it.

★ Keep a record of updated changes.

★ If the request is either unreasonable or not feasible, explain patiently. (Communicate with tourists patiently and privately, reducing unnecessary trouble and misunderstanding. Or let the tour leader or national guide help explain to the tourists. Always avoid confrontation with tourists.)

旅游团的旅游者背景各不相同，在不同的情况下不同的客人会有不同的要求。在处理旅游者个人诉求时，导游要遵循以下基本原则：

☆ 认真倾听。（在旅游者面前表现出你很关注他们的诉求是非常重要的。即便旅游者的要求不合理，也不宜断然拒绝，旅游者会因此认为你不关心他们。）

☆ 分析旅游者的要求是否合理可行。（导游可以咨询领队或全陪，因为行程中他们一直与旅游者在一起，对客人更加了解。）

☆ 如果旅游者的要求既合理又可行，及时报告旅行社积极安排。

☆ 改变后的计划记录备案。

☆ 如果旅游者的要求不合理或不可行，耐心解释。（私下与旅游者沟通，减少不必要的麻烦和误会。也可以让领队或全陪帮助解释。尽量避免与旅游者发生正面冲突。）

【备注】对待旅游者个别要求的原则是合理而可行。通常个别要求处理有两种结果：其一，合理而可行，则帮助安排；其二，合理而不可行或可行而不合理，则委婉拒绝，耐心解释。

124. What will you do when a tourist wants to end his/her tour ahead of schedule?（如旅游者想提前结束行程，导游应如何处理？）

★ If his/her health does not allow him/her to continue the trip or something urgent is happening back at home, try your best to help him/her.

★ Report the case to the agency to get further assistance (such as getting the visa separated from the group one, booking/buying the return ticket, etc.).

★ Explain to the tourist that all additional charges after the conclusion of the tour are to be covered by the tourist, payable on demand.

★ Tell the tourist he/she can talk to his/her travel agent about travel insurance claims and the possibility of a refund on any unused portions.

★ Sincerely express that you would be delighted to show him/her around again if he/she comes back one day.

☆ 如旅游者因身体原因或家中急事需提前结束行程，应尽力为其提供方便。

☆ 将此事及时通知旅行社（以协助其办理分离签证、

购买回程票等事宜）。

☆ 告诉旅游者，离团后一切费用自理。

☆ 告诉旅游者与自己的旅游代理商联系，了解关于旅游保险费用和旅游合同中未产生费用的退赔事宜。

☆ 表达旅游者日后重返时可以再次担任他/她的导游的愿望。

【备注】因提前结束行程而出现的费用退返问题，导游不便也不要回应。建议旅游者直接咨询自己的旅游代理商。

125. What will you do if a tourist wants to change his/her room for a better view?（如旅游者要求换景观房，导游应如何处理？）

★ Contact the hotel reception desk to inform them of his/her request (figuring out whether there are rooms available and the price difference).

★ Accompany him/her to the reception desk to change one after he/she agrees to cover the difference if there is any.

★ Then make the new room number known to the tour leader.

★ Inform the bell captain to help the tourist move to the new room.

★ Ask for copies of the new rooming list to be sent to the tour leader and the bell captain.

★ If the request can not be satisfied, explain patiently.

☆ 告知前台旅游者换房要求（了解是否有房及房间差价）。

☆ 如有差价，在其同意付差价后，陪同旅游者前往前台联系调换。

☆ 告知领队旅游者的新房间号码。

☆ 通知礼宾部协助旅游者搬至新房间。

☆ 通知前台将更改后的入住名单送至领队和礼宾部。

☆ 如无法满足旅游者要求，耐心解释，取得谅解。

126. How will you handle the incident that rooms provided by the travel agency are below the standard specified in the contract?（如因旅行社提供的客房低于合同规定标准，旅游者提出要求调换房间，导游应如何处理？）

★ The travel agency should fulfill the contract and change rooms for tourists.

★ If there are any difficulties, reasons should be clearly stated and an apology should be made.

★ Tell tourist the compensation provided by the travel agency.

★ A consent declaration with signatures of all tourists and the tour leaders is required.

☆ 这种情况旅行社应负责予以调换。

☆ 如果确有困难须说明原因并致歉。

☆ 按旅行社意见告知补偿措施。

☆ 并征得全体旅游者的书面同意。

【备注】如因客房内设施损坏、卫生不达标、房间有异味等原因而提出的换房要求，导游也应积极联系、满足换房要求。《旅游法》第七十五条规定：住宿经营者应当按照旅游服务合同的约定为团队游客提供住宿服务。住宿经营者未能按照旅游服务合同提供服务的，应当为游客提供不低于原定标准的住宿服务，因此增加的费用由住宿经营者承担；但由于不可抗力、政府因公共利益需要采取措施造成不能提供服务的，住宿经营者应当协助安排游客住宿。

127. What should the tour guide do when some tourists insist on moving to rooms which are above the standard stipulated in the contract? （如旅游者要求住高于合同规定标准的房间，导游应如何处理？）

★ Make sure tourists know and agree that all expenses incurred are to be covered by themselves.

★ Help them contact the hotel directly.

★ If there are rooms available, help them change rooms and report it to the travel agency.

★ If required rooms are not available, the tour guide should explain patiently.

☆ 确认旅游者知晓并同意因此产生的费用由其自理。

☆ 帮助旅游者直接与宾馆方面联系。

☆ 如有空房，可予以满足，事后把情况汇报给旅行社。

☆ 如没有空房间，导游要向旅游者解释清楚，取得谅解。

【备注】如旅游者有此要求，提醒旅游者将产生额外费用并协助旅游者与宾馆直接沟通。由宾馆直接告知并收取将产生的确切费用，操作更直接透明。如旅游者的要求涉及更换更高规格的酒店，导游应与领队配合，尽力说服客人住在合同约定的酒店。

128. What should the tour guide do if tourists propose to change the attraction specified in the contract to another?（如旅游者提出更改某一景点，导游应如何处理？）

The request can only be satisfied under the following four conditions:

★ It is the request of the whole group; the tour leader (the national guide) has no objection to it.

★ Time permits.

★ All tourists agree to pay the extra expense if there are any.

★ A written application with signatures of all tourists should be submitted.

★ Then report the case to the office.

★ Well arrange the new program.

改变行程单中的景点需满足以下四个条件：

☆ 全体旅游者共同要求，领队无异议。

☆ 时间许可。

☆ 全体旅游者同意更换所引起的费用自理。

☆ 旅游者提出书面申请并签名。

☆ （满足上述条件的前提下）报告旅行社。

☆ 导游做好新景点游览安排。

【备注】《旅游法》第七十三条规定：旅行社根据游客的具体要求安排旅游行程，与游客订立包价旅游合同的，旅游者请求变更旅游行程安排，因此增加的费用由游客承担，减少的费用退还旅游者。(According to Article 73 of *Tourism Law*: The travel agency shall make travel arrangements following specific requirements of the tourists; in case the travel agency has signed a package tourism contract, yet the tourists request changing the travel arrangements, which then incurs additional fees, such fees shall be borne by the tourists, and the reduced fees shall be returned to the tourists.) 增加景点与更换景点的处理方法类同。

129. What will you do if one tourist wants to skip part of the program?（如旅游者想放弃部分景点，导游应如何处理？）

★ Kindly suggest the tourist stay with the group.

★ If the tourist insists, make sure that the tourist knows what he/she is going to skip, so there are no regrets later.

★ Let the tourist know that there are no refunds on any unused portion of the tour, including meals.

★ Upon request, recommend some places that he/she might be interested in and possibly wish to explore.

★ Remind the tourist to take care of himself/herself when he/she is away from the group.

★ Leave him/her your cell phone number in case he/she need assistance.

☆ 建议旅游者随团活动。

☆ 如旅游者坚持，提醒旅游者他/她将放弃什么景点，以免后悔。

☆ 告诉旅游者，他/她放弃的景点和餐费是不能退款的。

☆ 应旅游者要求，向其推荐他/她可能会感兴趣并自行游览的地方。

☆ 告知旅游者其离团期间的安全注意事项。

☆ 将联系方式留给旅游者，以备不时之需。

130. What will you do if most of the tour members want to skip one tourist attraction in the itinerary, but there are still tourists who want to keep the original program?（如大多数旅游者希望取消行程安排中的某一景点，但仍有少数旅游者要求按照原行程活动，导游应如何处理？）

★ Emphasize the importance of keeping the contract.

(Explain to the whole group that the tour functions according to the agreed itinerary as it is their purchased product and is part of the contract. The guide is in no position to change it.)

★ Try to arouse their interests. (Tell tourists how long the tour is and let them know about what they might find interesting if they stay with you.)

★ Even if there is only one tourist who wants to keep the original program, you must stay with him/her.

☆ 向旅游者说明按照合同办事的重要性。（告知行程上的一切景点都是他们事先购买的旅游产品，是旅游合约的一部分，导游无权私自更改。）

☆ 想方设法引起旅游者的兴趣。（告诉旅游者该景点的游览时间，并让他们知道如果跟随导游，也许还会有出乎意料的收获。）

☆ 即使只有一名旅游者坚持原来行程，导游也要安排。

【备注】在此情况下，即便因忽略大多数旅游者的诉求而受到投诉，导游也不用因此承担责任。在实际操作中，导游可根据具体情况灵活安排，这也是考验导游的协调组织能力的时候。《旅游法》第四十一条规定：导游和领队应当严格执行旅游行程安排，不得擅自变更旅游行程或者中止服务活动，不得向游客索取小费，不得诱导、欺骗、强迫或者变相强迫旅游者购物或者参加另行付费旅游项目。(According to Article 41 of *Tourism Law*: Tour guides and tour leads shall strictly follow the itinerary, shall not alter it or stop the services they are providing without permission or to ask for tips from tourists or lure, cheat, compel or force tourists in a disguised form to make purchases or participate in tourism activities that require additional payment.)

131. How will the tour guide handle the request of changing transportation means?（如旅游者要求更换交通工具，导游应如何处理？）

★ Emphasize the importance of keeping the contract and try to persuade tourists politely and patiently.

★ If there are special reasons, report to the office.

★ Let tourists know that they should cover extra expense if there are any.

★ If the travel agency agrees on tourists' proposal, sign a new contract after tourists submit a written application with their signatures.

★ Keep a record.

☆ 告知旅游者遵守旅游合同约定的重要性。礼貌婉拒，耐心说服。

☆ 旅游者如有特殊情况，请示旅行社。

☆ 告知旅游者，如引发额外费用，由旅游者承担。

☆ 如旅行社同意，应由旅游者提出书面申请并签名，重新订立合同。

☆ 做好记录。

132. What should a tour guide do if a tourist in an overseas group wants to invite a friend in Shanghai to join the group to Beijing?（如境外旅游团有位旅游者想邀请在上海的朋友一起随团到北京旅游，导游应如何处理？）

★ Communicate with the tour leader and get the consent of the tour leader and the whole group.

★ The travel agency agrees.

★ Help the tourist go through such formalities as providing valid documents, filling out the form and paying for the tour.

★ After participating in the group, the new tourist should be treated with the same care and concern.

★ Make sure the office has arranged accommodation and bought ticket for the new tourist.

★ Make sure the office inform the next stop of this issue.

★ If the request cannot be met, explain patiently.

☆ 导游应首先征得领队和全团其他成员同意。

☆ 征得旅行社同意。

☆ 为该朋友办理加入旅游团的手续：如出示有效证件、填写表格、交纳费用。

☆ 参加团队后，讲清注意事项，与其他成员一视同仁。

☆ 提醒旅行社为其订房、订餐、订票。

☆ 提醒旅行社通知下一站人数变动。

☆ 如无法满足，做好解释工作。

【备注】如请求随团的亲友或朋友是驻华使馆、领馆人员，应告知旅游者邀请须征得本地外事部门同意，方可办理。

133. How should the tour guide do if a tourist asks him/her to help pass a parcel on to a friend?（如旅游者委托导游协助转递物品，导游应如何处理？）

★ Ask the tourist to write an engagement letter including detailed description of the parcel and the contact information of the receiver.

★ Make sure the description in the engagement letter is in agreement with the parcel.

★ Help pass the parcel on to the receiver and ask him to write a receipt with details concerning the parcel.

★ Leave the engagement letter and the receipt to the travel agency.

★ Inform the tourist.

☆ 请旅游者写出委托书，写明物品及接收人的详细信息。

☆ 核对物品，看是否与委托书一致。

☆ 帮助转交，要办好签收手续，请收件人写出收据，并详细注明所收物品情况。

☆ 将委托书和收据送交旅行社保管。

☆ 及时通知旅游者。

【备注】遇到此类要求，尽量拒绝。现在快递服务很方便，实际操作中不建议为客人转递物品，因为过程、手续比较麻烦。应旅游者要求，可介绍可靠的快递公司提供服务。另外，凡是食品、药品、贵重物品或违禁物品，应果断拒绝。

134. If a tourist wants to buy something, but unfortunately it is currently out of stock. He/She asks you to assist in the purchase and arrange for the shipment when it is available. What is the best way to deal with this situation?（如旅游者所需商品暂时缺货，旅游者请求导游代为购买并邮寄，如何处理比较妥当？）

★ Suggest that the tourist have direct contact with the shop manager through E-mail to discuss the details of the price, payment, shipment and delivery. Then, they can finish the transaction online.

★ Exchange E-mail addresses with the tourist, in case there are any complications that require further communication.

☆ 建议旅游者直接找商店经理商量，回国后通过网上联络，进一步讨论价格、支付方式以及托运方式，最终完成网上交易。

☆ 与旅游者互留电邮地址，以防日后旅游者需要帮助。

【备注】代为购买的传统操作一般需请示旅行社，获得同意后，请旅游者写委托书，留充足费用，代为购买并托运，所有单据原件寄送旅游者，复印件留存旅行社。事实上，现在购物很方便，许多商家接受网络支付，交易一般可在网上完成。因此，不建议导游为旅游者代购商品，因为过程比较复杂。

Related words and phrases

contact address	联系地址
complaint box	意见箱
seat by number	对号入座
occupied	（洗手间）有人
vacant	（洗手间）无人
luggage elevator	行李电梯
luggage receipt	行李收据
paid consumption	有偿消费
laundry service	洗衣服务
service charge	服务费
cancel the reservation	取消预订
commission fee/charge	手续费
safety precautions	安全提示

Questions for discussion

1. As a local tour guide, how will you respond to the request of a tourist who chooses to stay out of a mountain-climbing activity?

2. How will you respond to a group of architects who would like an add-on visit to Zhujiajiao in Shanghai for it's well-preserved traditional housing?
3. What will you do when the tour leader asks you to add on a new spot?

听力音频

Unit 14 Handling Emergencies and Common Issues 突发事件和常见问题的处理

135. What are the principles of dealing with unexpected problems?（发生旅游事故时，导游的处理原则是什么？）

★ Figure out the situation.

★ Handle the emergency in time and minimize the risks and loss.

★ Report to the office, waiting for instructions.

★ Well arrange the remaining programs according to the instructions of the travel agency.

★ Keep a record.

☆ 摸清情况，找出故障环节。

☆ 及时处理，力求减少损失。

☆ 报告旅行社，等待指令。

☆ 根据旅行社指示，做好后续活动安排。

☆ 写出事故报告。

136. What are the common reasons which may lead to the change of itinerary?（常见的旅游计划变更的原因有哪些？）

★ Changes due to the requirements of the group or tourists for various reasons.

★ The group encountering force majeure such as bad weather, natural disasters and traffic problems.

★ Changes due to mistakes made by the travel agency.

☆ 因各种原因，旅游团（旅游者）要求更改旅游计划。

☆ 因遭遇不可抗力因素（如气候变化、自然灾害、交通故障等）引发的旅游计划变更。

☆ 旅行社方面工作出错引发的旅游计划更改。

【备注】遭遇无法控制的情况应被视为不可抗力，包括但不限于火灾、风灾、水灾、地震、爆炸、叛乱、传染、检疫、隔离。(Any event or circumstance beyond control should be regarded as force majeure but not restricted to fire, wind, flood earthquake, explosion, rebellion, epidemic quarantine and segregation.)

137. What will you do if you find that the tourists' itinerary is different from yours?（如导游手中日程与旅游者的日程不符，应如何处理？）

★ Report it to the office right away and wait for the solution to the problem.

★ If the local travel agency is responsible for the problem, the local guide should explain and apologize honestly and sincerely.

★ If the mistake is due to other parties, the local guide should work with the tour leader and ask the tour leader to explain to the group.

☆ 立即向旅行社报告，等待指示。

☆ 倘若责任在我方，导游应实事求是地说明情况，并致歉。

☆ 倘若非我方责任，导游应与领队共同解决，可请领队做好解释工作。

【备注】作为导游，授权有限，遇到上述情况不可急于辩解，可以说："出现了这样的事很遗憾，我会立即汇报，相信很快会有一个说法。"（"I am sorry. I don't know what is wrong with the program. I will call the office right away. Pretty soon, we will get the answer."）简而言之，遇此类问题应首先弄清情况：如属地接社责任，地陪代表地接社道歉；如非地接社责任，地陪协助解决。

138. If you fail to arrive at the airport on time to greet the tourists due to personal reasons, what will you do to make up for the mistake?（如果导游因个人原因未能及时抵达机场迎接旅游者，应如何弥补过失？）

★ Make a sincere apology to tourists. Never make up an

excuse to cover up a mistake.

★ Promise to make extra efforts to provide good service to win the trust of tourists again.

★ If necessary, offer some small gifts to tourists.

★ Stay with the group unless the tourists insist on changing a new guide due to your mistake.

☆ 向旅游者诚恳道歉，切不可随意编造理由来掩饰自身失误。

☆ 承诺会加倍努力提供优质服务，以重新赢得旅游者的信任。

☆ 必要时，酌情给旅游者一定的物质补偿，如赠送小礼品。

☆ 如旅游者没有因此事坚持更换导游，导游应继续提供服务。

139. A tour guide found he picked up a wrong group when he was helping the tour leader check in at the hotel. What should the tour guide do?（如在办理酒店入住手续时才发现接错了团，导游应如何处理？）

★ Report to the office and ask the office to investigate the case.

★ If these two groups belong to the same agency, the tour guides have to make the best of this situation and stay with the wrongly-picked groups.

★ If they belong to different agencies, the tour guides should exchange groups as soon as possible.
★ Explain to the group and make a sincere apology.
★ Keep a record.

☆ 报告旅行社，请其协助查明具体情况。
☆ 如果错接发生在本社的两个旅游团之间，两名导游将错就错，将接待计划交换后继续接团。
☆ 如果错接的旅游团是两家不同旅行社的，尽快交换旅游团。
☆ 实事求是说明情况并致歉。
☆ 做好事件记录。

140. How will you handle the loss of luggage at the port of entry?（如何处理在入境口岸行李丢失？）

★ If the luggage is found missing at the port of entry, make sure that the tourist has filled out the airline's missing luggage form and has the name of the airline person in charge and his/her contacting telephone number.
★ Inform the tourist that you will keep in contact with the airline while he/she is in your city.
★ Help the tourist get things that are needed before the luggage is located (such as small items of daily necessities).
★ If the missing luggage fails to show up before the group leaves your city, inform the travel company or the next

stop to trace the luggage.

★ After the group leaves, keep a record of all related situations.

☆ 如旅游者在入境口岸没有拿到行李，确保旅游者已填写航空公司提供的行李遗失表格并留有联系人姓名及电话号码。

☆ 告诉旅游者在团队逗留期间，你会与航空公司保持联系。

☆ 协助旅游者购买急需用品（通常是日用品）。

☆ 如在旅行团离开你所在的城市之前，行李仍未找到，通知组团社或下一站地接社，以便继续追踪行李去向。

☆ 旅游团离开后，做好相关记录备案。

【备注】入境口岸行李丢失，通常领队会协助旅游者填写相关表格（包括行李运输事故记录单 PIR，记录单上设有“延误行李登记编号”，可通过编号自行上网查询行李进度）。导游在协助旅游者购买急需用品时，正常情况下不要替旅游者支付费用，因为相关的保险赔付会直接打进被保险人登记的银行账号。向旅游者说明情况，并请旅游者自行支付相关费用。行李查找一般需要 21 天，如果 21 天后行李仍未找到，旅客有权提出索赔要求。

141. How will you handle the loss of personal belongings?（如何处理旅游者个人物品丢失？）

★ Comfort the tourist, and find out the details of the case. If the loss is confirmed, report the case to the local travel agency and the local police station. Certain document should be well kept.

★ Upon the request of the tourist, the local travel agency can produce a written statement with the signature of the local guide as a witness.

★ Write down the tourist's address for further contact.

☆ 安抚旅游者情绪，了解事件始末细节。如确认丢失，报告旅行社及当地警察局。保管好相关材料。

☆ 应旅游者要求，地接社可出具书面说明，导游签字为证。

☆ 请旅游者留下联系方式以备日后联系。

【备注】不少国外旅游者在来华前，购买了多种保险，凭证明可回去要求索赔。中国国家旅游局《旅行社旅客旅游意外保险实施细则》对此规定是：旅客的个人物品在其个人照管或携带时丢失，保险公司不予赔偿；如在饭店、交通工具内丢失的，须有该饭店、运输部门的保卫部门或有关公安局报案证明，有了以上证明，保险公司可以受理赔付。因此，旅游者在旅游期间要妥善保管好自己携带的财物，一旦发现财物失窃，应及时报案，并取得有关部门出具的立案证明，有了立案证明，旅行社即可凭此为旅游者向保险公司申请理赔。没有立案证明，旅行社对旅游者随身携带的财物损坏或遗失不负向保险公司申请理赔的责任。

142. If a tourist can't locate his/her passport, what kind of help can you offer?（如旅游者遗失护照，导游可以提供哪些帮助？）

★ Call the places where the tourist has been to, like restaurants, theaters or tourist attractions…

★ Suggest that the tourist check with the hotel's duty manager to see if it has been turned in. Look in all the places he/she has been to in the hotel including the tourist's own room.

★ If all efforts are in vain, you should share the following procedures with the tourist and assist him/her to obtain a new passport:

Step 1: Report the loss of passport to the local police station and get a valid written proof of statement.

Step 2: Get a "Proof of Personal Identity as a Tourist" from the local travel agency.

Step 3: Present all necessary documents, including those mentioned above, to the local Entry and Exit Management of Public Security Bureau, and get a certificate of loss.

Step 4: With the certificate and a few recently taken photos (the exact number depends on the issuing country), the tourist is able to apply for a new passport from that country's closest consulate or the embassy in Beijing.

Step 5: Get a visa on the new passport from the local Entry

& Exit Administration of the Public Security Bureau.

Step 6: Clarify with the tourist, as soon as possible, that all the expenses incurred are the responsibility of the tourist.

☆ 打电话到旅游者去过的场所，诸如饭店、剧场、旅游景点等地查找。

☆ 建议旅游者找酒店大堂经理寻求协助，在酒店内部仔细查找，包括旅游者的房间。

☆ 如无结果，地陪应该按以下程序协助旅游者补办新护照：

第一步：向当地警察局报失，开具有效报失证明。

第二步：由旅行社出具旅游者旅游身份证明。

第三步：向当地公安局出入境管理机构递交以上证明，获取护照遗失证明。

第四步：携带护照遗失证明和近期标准照片若干张（具体照片张数各国有不同的要求）前往旅游者所在国驻中国大使馆或领事馆申办新护照。

第五步：凭新护照到当地公安局出入境管理机构办理新的签证。

第六步：及时告知旅游者一切费用自理。

【备注】大使馆（embassy）是一国在建交国首都派驻的常设外交代表机关。领事馆（consulate）是一国政府派驻对方国家某个城市并在一定区域执行领事职务的政府代表机关。大使馆的职责范围遍及驻在国各个地区，领事馆只负责某一管辖地区。港澳同胞来内地后遗失港澳通行证应向遗失地的市、县或者交通运输部门的公安机关报失，经公安机关调查属实，出具证明，由公安机关出入境管理部门签发一次有效的《中华人民共和国出入境通行证》，凭证返回香港、澳门。台湾游客一旦遗失旅行证件，应立即到遗失地的市、县公安机关报失，也可以到发现遗失地的公安机关报失，凭报失证明向当地市、县公安机关出入境管理部门申请补领旅行证件。经公安机关出入境管理部门核查属实的，允许重新申请领取相应的旅行证件，或予以补发一次出境有效的《台湾居民来往大陆通行证》。

如考题考查如何补办护照，则直接回答一到六步，寻找环节省略；如考题的描述为游客找不到护照，则应加上寻找环节。

143. How will you deal with the problem that a tourist fails to get his luggage?（如旅游者进房一段时间后没有拿到行李，导游应如何处理？）

★ Go to the hotel concierge with the tour leader to see whether the luggage was sent to the wrong floor or wrong room.

★ If the total number of luggage arriving at the hotel is not the same as the figure written on the luggage tag, call the local agency to trace the lost piece.

★ While tracing the luggage, comfort the tourist and offer assistance if it is needed.

★ If the loss is confirmed, apologize and help with compensation.

☆ 与领队去酒店礼宾部，查询行李是否送错楼层或房间。

☆ 如果酒店在接收行李时的总数与行李牌上的数目不符，电话联系地接社请其协助查询丢失行李。

☆ 在寻找行李的过程中，安抚好旅游者，协助解决因行李丢失带来的困难。

☆ 如行李确认丢失，表示歉意并由责任方赔偿。

【备注】如行李不是礼宾部负责运送，导游可与领队一同去团队其他成员房间寻找，看行李是否有误拿。行李追踪的基本原则是“由近到远”。

144. What will you do if one of the tourists refuses to share a standard room with another tourist due to conflicts or different living habits?（如住同一标间的两位旅游者因闹矛盾或生活习惯不同而要求住单间，导游应如何处理？）

★ Work with the tour leader and try to solve the problem in the group.

★ If no one wants to change rooms with them, and if there are rooms available, the tour guide should help them change rooms.

★ The tour guide should tell them in advance that the one who insists on changing rooms is responsible for the extra expense.

☆ 导游首先应请领队调解或在内部调整。

☆ 若调解调配不成，且酒店有空房，可满足其要求。

☆ 导游要事先说明，房费由旅游者自理，一般是谁坚持住单间谁付房费。

【**备注**】因房间调换涉及的费用，请旅游者签字为证并现付。通常的支付原则是“谁提出，谁支付”。

145. If a tourist falls ill, what services will you provide?（如旅游者生病，导游应如何处理？）

★ Never offer medicine to the tourist.

★ If the tourist agrees, send him/her to the hospital immediately.

★ Report the case to the office. Make sure that the tourist is well cared for in the hospital.

★ If an operation is needed, contact the tour leader to get the approval of his/her direct relatives upon the request of the hospital.

★ If the tourist has to leave the group and cancel the rest of the trip, all questions concerning travel insurance claims and the possibility of a refund for the unused portions of the trip should be directed to his/her travel agent.

★ After the group leaves, offer assistance to the tourist and make sure that he/she leaves the city safe and sound.

★ Keep a record.

☆ 导游不得擅自向旅游者提供药品。

☆ 经旅游者同意，立即将其送院治疗。

☆ 向旅行社汇报事件进展并与医院保持联系，以确保患者得到良好照顾。

☆ 如需手术，导游应协助院方通过领队获得旅游者直系亲属的同意并签字。

☆ 如旅游者因病必须离团并取消剩余行程，告知他/她可以与自己的旅游代理人取得联系，商量旅游保险索赔和旅游合同中未产生费用的退款事宜。

☆ 旅行团离开后，导游应继续为住院旅游者提供相应帮助，直至旅游者安全离开。

☆ 做好事件记录。

【备注】现在患者入院，基本都会由懂英文的医生和护士照料，没有语言沟通问题。大城市还有外国人开的医院。签证也一般在私人护照上，不用分离；如涉及签证到期，应向当地公安局出入境管理处寻求帮助。旅游者可以使用信用卡结算费用，基本不用导游或旅行社垫付。旅游者来华前基本都买了旅游保险，回去后可与保险公司交涉。导游应提醒领队保留所有就诊原始凭据，并协助领队完成出险经过和情况说明。

146. What measures can be taken to prevent tourists from getting sick?（导游带团时应采取何种措施预防旅游者患病？）

★ The tour guide should have a general idea of the health condition of the group.

★ Well arrange programs, controlling the pace of the group.

★ Forecast weather and remind them to take care of themselves (suitable clothes and necessary medicine).

★ Remind them to pay attention to food hygiene and discourage them to eat food in small stalls and roadside stalls.

★ Pay special attention to the elderly, children, and the disabled.

☆ 导游应随时掌握旅游者的健康状况。

☆ 安排游览时要注意节奏，劳逸结合。

☆ 坚持每天向旅游者播报天气情况，及时嘱咐旅游者增减衣服和随身携带防护用品。

☆ 提醒旅游者注意饮食卫生，不吃大排档和路边摊。

☆ 对老年人、小孩、残疾人要多加照顾提醒。

147. If a tourist suffers from heatstroke, how will you handle the situation?（如有旅游者中暑，导游应如何处理？）

★ Let the tourist lie down in a shaded area and put a wet towel on his/her forehead.

★ Offer him/her some cold water (ice-cold water) and let him/her have a short rest.

★ If the tourist still feels unwell, escort him/her to the hotel and ask the hotel staff to take care of him/her; or send him/her to the hospital if he/she wants.

★ Call the tourist once in a while to see whether he/she needs more help.

☆ 让中暑旅游者在阴凉处躺下，将湿毛巾敷于其前额。
☆ 为旅游者提供凉水（冰水），让其进行短暂休息。
☆ 如旅游者依然感觉不适，可将其送回酒店，请酒店给予照顾；或经本人同意，送医院治疗。
☆ 与旅游者保持联系，以便提供帮助。

【备注】高热、无汗及昏迷是中暑的特征性症状。对于先兆中暑、轻症中暑，如处理及时，往往可短时间内恢复。对于重症中暑，要即刻送医院救治。通常导游继续带团，领队和家属送游客去酒店或医院，如有必要，可联系办公室，请办公室派人协助。

148. What preventive measures will you take to avoid heatstroke among tourists?（为预防旅游者中暑，导游应采取哪些防范措施？）

★ During the hot summer, avoid conducting the tour under the scorching sun for a long time.

★ When outdoor activities are a must, remind tourists to bring such things as sunhats, sun umbrellas, and sunglasses. Always find a place with shade for people to take a short rest and condense the outdoor informationsharing sessions — part of them can be said on the coach before or after the tour.

★ Take breaks once in a while, so tourists can rest and replenish liquids.

★ Inform tourists that if they need help, don't hesitate to let you know.

☆ 在炎热夏季，避免长时间在烈日下活动。

☆ 如无法避免户外活动，提醒旅游者带上防暑物品，如遮阳帽、遮阳伞、太阳镜等。尽量多安排旅游者在阴凉处做短暂逗留并压缩讲解内容，部分景点信息可以事先或事后在车上提供。

☆ 适时安排途中短暂休息，以方便旅游者补充饮用水。

☆ 让旅游者知道，如需帮助，应及时告知导游。

【备注】中暑的因素除了气温外，还跟湿度、日照、运动强度、高温环境下暴露时间、体质强弱、营养状况、水盐供给以及个体健康状况有关。年老、体弱多病、怀孕、肥胖、饥饿也都可能是中暑的原因。

149. How will you deal with the incident that a tourist suffers from sudden angina pectoris during the tour?（如旅游者在游览途中突发心绞痛，导游应如何处理？）

★ Let him/her lie down or sit down.

★ Check if the tourist has any emergency medication.

Ask his/her relatives or the tour leader to look for the medicine and help the patient take it.

★ Call 120 and send the tourist to the hospital if necessary.

★ If the tourist stops breathing or the heart stops, immediately perform CPR until medical personnel arrive.

☆ 立即让患者停止活动，躺下或坐下。

☆ 了解患者是否随身携带了急救药物。如带有药物，请患者亲属或领队找出并协助患者服用。

☆ 如需要，应及时联系 120，送医院治疗。

☆ 如突发心跳呼吸停止，立即做心外按摩和人工呼吸，直至医护人员到达。

【备注】患有此类疾病的旅游者通常会随身携带药物。心绞痛的特征是阵发性胸前区压榨性疼痛，常发生在劳累、寒冷环境或者情绪激动时，胸痛持续时间大多为 5~15 分钟，经休息或服用硝酸甘油可缓解。严重者要争取在第一时间送往有心脏专科的医院，延误可导致心肌细胞不可逆死亡、心肌梗死。一位全国知名的导游在接受访谈时，曾被问及对此种情形的处理，他的回答是：每次出长线，此类药物会准备。在被问及是否会担心提供药物会惹来不必要的麻烦时，他说，在生命和责任的选择中，他选择前者。这是一件令很多导游为难的事。但在考试中，回答此问题时，建议坚持不擅自给旅游者提供药物的说法。

150. What will you do if a tourist trips and injures his ankle causing bleeding and swelling?（如旅游者在游览途中不慎摔跤，脚踝处出血肿痛，导游应如何处理？）

★ Help stop bleeding.

★ Bind up the wound.

★ The knee and ankle joints must be immobilized.

★ Send the tourist to hospital.

☆ 协助止血。

☆ 包扎。

☆ 固定，下肢骨折要固定两个关节以上。

☆ 送医院。

【备注】受伤旅游者的医疗费用由本人支付，后续按照有关保险规定处理。为骨折伤员固定伤处，力求稳妥牢固。骨折的固定一般是需要固定上下两个关节。对有可能是颈椎、脊柱骨折的旅游者，注意固定和搬运方法，确保安全，避免再度损伤。骨折临时固定器材分为制式器材和就便器材。就便器材有木板、木棍、树枝、竹竿、床单、毛巾、衣物、布袋、绳子等。导游应具备基本的急救知识，以应对可能出现的紧急状况。

151. How will you deal with the incident that a tourist shows signs of altitude sickness?（如旅游者有高原反应，导游应如何处理？）

★ Let the tourist take oxygen.

★ Ask the tourist to have high-sugar drinks; ask him/her not to take salty drinks.

★ If necessary, send the tourist to hospital for further treatment.

☆ 吸氧。

☆ 补充高糖饮料，忌含盐饮料。

☆ 严重者送医院治疗。

【备注】高原反应的常见症状包括：头痛、失眠、食欲减退、疲倦、呼吸困难等。头痛是最常见的症状，其发生概率，老年人低于年轻人，女性低于男性。

152. Are there any tips which are helpful for overcoming altitude sickness?（如何帮助旅游者预防高原反应？）

★ Tourist should get a health checkup before the trip.

★ Take some medicine (like Rhodiola) a week before departure.

★ Keep warm in order not to catch a cold.

★ Do not run or walk quickly.

★ Refrain from drinking alcohol, smoking or overeating.

☆ 旅行出发前，做一次体检。
☆ 出发前一周，开始服用相关药物（如红景天）。
☆ 注意保暖，避免感冒。
☆ 不要跑也不要快速行走。
☆ 不要喝酒吸烟，不要暴饮暴食。

【备注】High blood pressure, heart disease, lung dysfunction, having a cold and cough are life-threatening in plateau. 高血压、心脏病、肺功能减退、感冒发热、咳嗽，在高原可能引发致命的危险。曾有旅游者在路遇石块挡道时，下车推搬石块，随后便出现持续剧烈头痛。故在高原地区旅游时，应避免一切形式的剧烈运动。

153. In case of fire, how can a tour guide react properly?（如遇到火灾，导游应如何应对？）

★ Keep calm.
★ Call 119 immediately. And tell the police the exact location of the fire, the severity of the situation, etc.
★ Inform all the tourists and the tour leader if possible.
★ Help with the evacuation.
★ If the situation is serious, the tour guide should encourage tourists to help themselves and each other.
★ After reaching a safe place, call the office and count the number of tourists.

★ Send the injured to hospital and comfort the rest.

★ When the cause of the fire is determined, ask the manager or the tour leader to make it known to all tourists.

★ Keep a record.

☆ 尽量保持冷静。

☆ 立即报警，拨打火警电话 119，务必讲清确切的起火地点、火势等情况。

☆ 尽可能通知所有旅游者与领队。

☆ 听从指挥，有序疏散。

☆ 如发现火势已蔓延开，鼓励引导旅游者自救和互救。

☆ 到达安全地点，通知旅行社并清点旅游者人数。

☆ 送伤者去医院，安抚其他旅游者。

☆ 火灾原因清楚后，请旅行社经理或领队告知全团。

☆ 做好记录。

【备注】临危不惧、头脑清醒、遇事不乱、处事果断、办事利索、积极主动、随机应变是导游处理意外事故时应有的品质。在重大旅游事故的处理上，上述品质有助于稳定旅游者情绪、快速应对危机，从而降低事故所带来的损失和伤害。但在重大旅游事故发生时，导游也要保护好自己，进退有度。

154. What will you do if the group has to end the tour ahead of schedule due to various reasons?（如何处理旅游团因故提前结束行程？）

★ If the decision is made in your city, inform the travel company through your office, so they are able to cancel the rest of the trip in time.

★ Inform the tour leader and try to get his support.

★ Inform some tourists who have high prestige in the group and try to win support of them.

★ With the help of these people, inform the group and try to win support of all tourists.

★ Try your best to show people as many highlights as possible in the program within the time limit.

★ Follow the instructions of the office and make the tour a good ending.

☆ 如果提前结束行程的决定是在当地临时做出的，通过地接社及时告知组团社，以便及时取消余下的行程。

☆ 告知领队，并积极取得领队的支持。

☆ 告知团队较有威望的团员，并积极取得他们的支持。

☆ 在上述人员的支持下，告知全团，尽量赢得谅解。

☆ 在旅游者逗留的有限时间内，尽量游览完日程中所有的项目。

☆ 协助做好收尾工作。

【备注】本题的处理原则是“各个击破”，或可幽默地理解为“擒贼先擒王”。

155. What measures can be taken in order to persuade tourists to accept the new itinerary when the original one is changed due to force majeure?（旅游团因不可抗力因素发生行程变更，导游应如何做好旅游者的说服工作？）

★ Inform the tour leader as soon as possible, and make sure you're on the same page.

★ Explain the situation to the key people in the group, ask for their support, and get their help in convincing the others.

★ Work together to persuade the whole group and get their understanding.

☆ 及时告知领队，统一意见。

☆ 向旅游团中重点人物说明情况，希望得到支持，并请其协助说服其他成员。

☆ 大家共同做好全团旅游者的说服工作，争取谅解。

【备注】大多数旅游者能够理解并接受因不可抗力因素导致的行程变更；少部分旅游者会过度维权，提出不合理要求。导游服务团队应果断、灵活，防止不良情绪蔓延，影响整个团队。必要时，可将《旅游法》中相关条例告知旅游者，说服旅游者遵守法律，合法维权。

156. What should a tour guide do when the group misses the plane?（如旅游团误机，导游应如何处理？）

★ Immediately report to the office, seeking assistance.

★ Apologize to tourists and comfort them.

★ Try to minimize the loss. (Contact the airport as soon as possible to see whether the group can take the next flight.)

★ If all efforts fail, arrange accommodation and sightseeing of the group during the detention.

★ Notify the next stop.

★ Submit a detailed report to the office (including analysis of causes and lessons learned).

★ Compensation should be given according to the instructions of the travel agency.

☆ 立即报告旅行社，请求协助。

☆ 向旅游者赔礼道歉，稳定情绪。

☆ 尽量减少损失。（尽快联系航空公司，看是否可搭乘下一航班离开。）

☆ 如当天无法解决，安排好该旅游团滞留期间的食宿、游览事宜。

☆ 通知下一站。

☆ 提交事故小结（包括原因分析、教训总结等）。

☆ 根据旅行社意见补偿或赔偿。

【备注】如机票上未印制“不可转签、不可退票”，导游应直接去航空公司服务台，请工作人员核实下一航班是否有足够空位。如有足够空位，安排旅游者搭乘下一航班。如不行，请旅行社联系是否可改乘其他交通工具前往下一站，如可行及时通知下一站联系人。旅行社团队机票因价格优惠，通常是“三不”机票，即“不退不改不换”。通常旅行团误机所带来的损失比较大，如后续行程涉及转机，后果更是严重，导游在此环节一定要倍加小心、留出足够时间。同时，个人在网上订机票时也应注意，网络订票快捷方便，选择此种方式订票时要认真阅读温馨提示，留意特价机票属于哪种性质，如属“三不”机票，一旦订票成功，没有回旋余地。(If there is no stamp on the tickets with the words “No transfer; No refund”, go directly to the airline service counter and talk to an airline representative or at an airline reception to see whether there are enough empty seats for the group to leave on the next flight. If seats are not available, contact with the office to see whether the group can change other means of transport to the next station. Inform the next stop.)

157. What can you do if the group misses the train?（如旅游团误了火车，导游应如何处理？）

★ Call the office and ask for help.

★ Inform the the next stop in time.

★ Locate the railway station manager on duty immediately, explain the situation and try to transfer the group to the next available train.

★ Locate the group’s checked-in luggage and learn how they will be transported.

★ When the group leaves, immediately update those concerned at the next stop.

★ Submit a report to the office and keep a record.

☆ 联系旅行社，寻求帮助。

☆ 第一时间通知下一站。

☆ 立即联系火车站当班经理，解释事由并请其设法安排下一班火车。

☆ 如有随原车托运行李，但旅游者没赶上车，了解行李的去向并妥善安排好行李的托运。

☆ 旅游团离开后，立即将具体情况通知下一站。

☆ 向旅行社提交事件报告并做好记录。

158. What should a tour leader/national guide do when the group has arrived, but the local guide fails to show up?（如旅游团抵达时无人接站，领队/全陪应如何处理？）

★ Contact the local travel agency or the local guide to figure out the situation.

★ Explain the situation in brief to tourists and promise to solve the problem as soon as possible.

★ If the local guide is held up by traffic and will get there soon, lead the group to a comfortable place where they can use the washroom or take a rest.

★ If there is no way to get a local guide due to the mistake of local travel agency, call the travel company to be authorized to solve the problem like hiring taxis to send tourists to the designated hotel first.

★ The extra expense incurred will be covered by the one who is responsible for the mistake.

☆ 联系地接社或地陪，查明原因。

☆ 向全体旅游者告知情况，承诺尽快解决问题。

☆ 如地陪因交通堵塞迟到，但会很快赶到，安排旅游者在附近有卫生间设施处做短暂休息。

☆ 如因地接社漏派地陪，又无法临时安排，向组团社汇报，并全权处理此事，如让出租车把旅游者先送往酒店。

☆ 事后，发生的费用由责任人承担。

【备注】漏接发生后，如安排出租车送客人去酒店，应第一时间要求地接社派人配合。领队应写好酒店地址及个人电话交给司机，并说明酒店下客处已有人等候付款。客人分乘多辆出租车前往酒店，领队要记下所有车牌号，并将车牌号发给在酒店等候的旅行社工作人员。领队跟随最后一批客人离开。

159. What should the tour leader/national guide do when the personal security or property of the tourist is damaged?（当旅游者人身或财产受到损害时，领队/全陪应如何处理？）

★ Comfort the tourist and calmly deal with the incident to avoid further loss or damage.

★ Report to the travel company right away and gather evidence.

★ The travel company (the tour leader) sometimes has to pay for the treatment of tourists first.

★ Assist tourists in claiming compensation.

☆ 安抚旅游者，冷静处理，避免损失和伤害扩大。

☆ 及时报告组团社并收集证据。

☆ 旅行社（领队）在某些情况下，可以为旅游者的救治垫付资金。

☆ 领队/全陪有协助旅游者索赔的义务。

160. How should the tour leader/national guide deal with sudden natural disasters like typhoons, snowstorms or earthquakes?（如遇台风、暴风雪或地震等突发自然灾难，领队/全陪应如何处理？）

★ Report to the office and call the emergency hotline.

★ Take care of tourists and move them to a safe place as soon as possible.

★ Contact Chinese embassy or consulate of the destination country (region).

★ Try to arrange all tourists to return to China as soon as possible.

★ Keep all necessary documentation for insurance claims.

☆ 立即向旅行社汇报，并及时拨打目的地国家或地区的救援电话。

☆ 妥善安排旅游者并尽快将他们转移到安全的地方。

☆ 联系目的地国家的中国大使馆或领事馆。

☆ 积极安排所有旅游者尽快安全回国。

☆ 保留好证据，以便进行保险索赔。

161. What should the tour leader/national guide do if tourists lose their luggage at the hotel?（如旅游者在酒店丢失行李，领队/全陪应如何处理？）

★ Get the detailed information of the lost luggage.

★ Coordinate with the hotel to search for the lost luggage, and let them know if the luggage is not found, the police will be contacted.

★ Help tourists buy some daily necessities.

★ Keep all necessary documentation and help with insurance claims.

☆ 落实行李中贵重物品的价值。

☆ 与酒店沟通协商寻找，如找不到则报警。

☆ 协助旅游者购买急需物品。

☆ 保留好证据，协助旅游者进行保险索赔。

162. What should a tour leader/national guide do when the flight is delayed?（如遇航班延误，领队/全陪应如何处理？）

★ Report the case to the office.

★ Inform tourists of the delay in time.

★ Comfort tourists and take care of those who need help.

★ Consult with the airline company to see whether there are remedial measures.

★ The tour leader/national guide should be familiar with relevant regulations and let tourists know these regulations in time.

★ In case tourists take irrational behaviors, the tour leader/national guide should inform them that they should protect legitimate rights in accordance to relevant regulations.

☆ 报告旅行社。

☆ 及时将航班延误的相关信息告知旅游者。

☆ 安抚旅游者，关心帮助需要照顾的旅游者。

☆ 积极与航空公司沟通，寻求补救措施。

☆ 领队/全陪应熟悉相关政策，并及时告知旅游者。

☆ 万一遇到旅游者情绪激动、行为失控，领队/全陪应劝说旅游者合法维权。

【备注】依据交通运输部2016年公布的《航班正常管理规定》，从2017年1月1日起，由于天气、突发事件、空中交通管制、安检等非承运人原因，造成航班在始发地延误或取消，承运人应协助旅客安排食宿，费用由旅客自理。由于航空公司自身原因，包括机务维护、航班调配、机组等造成航班在始发地延误或取消，航空公司应当向旅客提供餐食或住宿等服务。航班在经停地延误或取消，无论何种原因，航空公司均应负责向经停旅客提供餐食或住宿服务。

不少旅游者购买的保险涵盖航班延误险。如遇航班延误，领队须在机场开具航班延误证明，包括航班号、原定航班时间、实际航班时间，延误客观原因、收集登机牌。如遇到机场不开具航班延误证明的情况，导游（领队）要打电话给保险公司报案，并对电子屏幕拍照留证。现在国内航班延误险一般都包含在意外险里面。航班延误险中有一种主动理赔的航班延误险，就是保险公司无须客户证明材料、通过系统自动跟踪被保险人延误情况并自动理赔的一种保险。

163. What should the tour leader do if a tourist does not return to China with the group?（如旅游者在境外滞留不归，领队应如何处理？）

★ Report to the office, contact the embassy or consulate of the destination country and inform the tourist's family.

★ When the group enters China, the tour leader should submit a detailed report.

★ Submit a detailed written report to the embassy, immigration, public security, and tourism authorities.

★ If the tourist returns home, make sure he/she report to relevant departments and close the case.

☆ 立即报告旅行社，联系目的地国家使领馆，并通知旅游者家属。

☆ 领队在回国入境时，须向边检递交情况说明。

☆ 向使馆、出入境管理处、公安机关、旅游主管部门进行书面汇报，陈述事情经过。

☆ 若滞留人员归国，告知其须向相关部门汇报并销案。

Related words and phrases

embassy	大使馆
consulate	领事馆
Public Security Bureau	公安局
report a case	报案
beware of pickpocket	谨防扒手
medical expenses	医药费
certificate of death	死亡证明
have one's visa extended	延长签证
have one's visa separated from the group visa	分离签证
emergency treatment	紧急处理
first aid	急救
reimbursement	赔偿
insurance	保险
food poisoning	食物中毒

food allergies	食物过敏
travel accident insurance	旅游意外险
the all-in-one package	综合服务（费）
stay abroad illegally	境外非法滞留
leave the group without permission	擅自离团

Questions for discussion

1. How would you respond to the incident that a tourist suddenly feels quite sick in a scenic spot?
2. A pious Christian tourist in your group hands out copies of the Bible and other religious souvenirs to the local people. As a local guide, what should you do?
3. What assistance can you offer to a tourist who wants to end the entire tour ahead of time because of an urgent call from home?
4. Your group has just finished a tour of Summer Palace. A tourist fails to arrive at the meeting point on time. 15 minutes have passed and your group gets impatient. As a local guide, what would you do to deal with such a case?

Part V The Art of Managing a Tour

导游带团艺术

听力音频

Unit 15 A Harmonious Service Team 和谐的服务团队

164. What are the differences between a tour leader, a national guide and a local guide?（领队、全陪、地陪有何区别？）

These three positions have different roles. The titles are not interchangeable.

★ A tour leader (also referred to as the tour escort in Central America, or tour conductor in Japan) is assigned by the foreign travel service to accompany the tour group through the whole trip. He/She accompanies the tour group from the passengers' point of departure to their safe return, and makes sure that the local travel agency fulfills the contract obligations. They work together with the local guide and sometimes a national guide as well.

★ A national guide (also known as a tour director or tour manager) is someone who leads a group throughout a country or part of a country. He/She is assigned by the travel company at the tourist destination. He/

She is in charge of the liaison work and supervises the implementation of the contract by the local travel agency.

★ A local guide, also referred to as a tour guide, is someone who works within an area they know very well. He/She is assigned by the local travel agency, meeting tourists and providing local guiding service.

三者名称不同，但却常常被混淆。

☆ 领队（在中美洲被称为“旅行陪同”，在日本被称为“观光领队”）是受海外旅行社委派，（代表该旅行社）带领旅游团从事旅游活动的工作人员。领队全程陪同旅游者，从出发直至安全返回，确保地接社按照合同提供各项服务。领队与地陪，有时还有全陪，合作共事。

☆ 全陪（也称为旅游经理）是为旅游团（者）提供国内全旅程陪同服务的导游人员。全陪受旅游目的地组团旅行社委派，负责联络工作，监督地接社按照合同实施接待计划。

☆ 地陪是在其熟悉的地区为旅行团（者）提供服务的人员。受地接社委派，迎接旅游团并为他们提供当地旅游活动安排。

【备注】目前中国旅游服务行业从业人员英语水平普遍提高，工作范围内的常规事宜基本可以用英语沟通解决，大部分入境旅行团为节约成本，基本采用领队与全陪的工作由一人承担的模式。海外旅行公司或自派领队，或要求组团社委派领队，弱化了全陪工作的职责与概念。故以下内容并未具体区分领队或全陪的工作职责。

165. What are the principles of establishing a good relationship between the local guide and the tour leader/national guide?（领队/全陪与地陪合作的要领有哪些？）

★ Respect each other's rights and interests.

★ Communicate frequently and establish good cooperative relations.

★ If you have different views in handling problems, discuss issues away from the group. Seek common ground.

★ If there are conflicts, settle them based on the contract.

★ If you fail to iron out disputes and narrow differences, report it to the office and wait for instruction from the agency.

☆ 尊重双方的权限和利益。

☆ 主动沟通，建立良好的协作关系。

☆ 如意见不同时，避免在旅游者前暴露矛盾，积极求同存异。

☆ 以协议为准，处置双方矛盾。

☆ 如无法解决争议或消除分歧，报告旅行社等待指示。

166. Under what circumstances, does a local guide need to consult with the tour leader/national guide?（地陪在哪些工作环节尤其需要与领队/全陪商榷沟通？）

★ When announcing the itinerary, the local guide should consult with the tour leader/national guide in advance. If there are no major differences, the local guide may adopt the views of the tour leader.

★ When the itinerary has to be changed due to various reasons, the local guide should consult with the tour leader/national guide first.

★ When dealing with emergencies, the tour leader/national guide's approval and help are indispensible.

☆ 地陪在公布活动日程前，一般应事先征求领队/全陪的意见，如无分歧，尽量考虑和采纳领队/全陪的意见。

☆ 旅游计划被迫更改时，地陪更要同领队/全陪进行磋商。

☆ 处理旅游紧急事件时，要得到领队/全陪的认可和帮助。

167. What are the common situations when the service team is consulting itinerary? What are the principles of dealing with such situations?（导游服务团队商榷日程安排时，常见的问题有哪些？如何处理这些问题？）

★ **Situation 1:** The tour leader suggests some minor changes to the itinerary or proposes adding new sightseeing activities.

If time permits and there is no additional charge involved, the guide may agree. If there is an additional charge involved, inform the tour leader and tourists and collect money in time. If time does not permit, explain patiently.

★ **Situation 2:** The request made by the tour leader is inconsistent with the original plan and involves change of reception standard. Politely refuse such requests. If there are special reasons, report to the office and wait for instructions.

★ **Situation 3:** The guide's itinerary is different from the tour leader's. Report to agency and figure out the reason. Solve the problem according to the instruction of the agency.

☆ 第一种情况：领队提出小的修改意见或增加新的游览项目。如时间上有保证、又不产生费用的情况下，可以同意；如需产生费用，应向领队和旅游者说明，按规定收取足够的费用；如时间不允许，耐心解释。

☆ 第二种情况：领队提出的要求与原计划不符又涉及接待规格。

婉言拒绝，并说明双方应按合同行事，但要做好解释工作；如有特殊理由，应请示组团旅行社。

☆ 第三种情况：导游手中的接待计划与领队的计划有部分不符。

报告旅行社查明原因，按照旅行社指示执行。

168. What should the tour leader/national guide do to cooperate with the local guide in providing a pleasant trip in each stop?（旅游团抵达某一城市后，领队/全陪需要在哪些方面配合地陪，做好服务工作？）

When arriving at the destination city, the tour leader/national guide should work with the local guide to fulfill the tourist contract. When providing service, the local tour guide usually plays a leading role while the tour leader/the national guide offers the following service.

★ Collect feedbacks of tourists during the trip.

★ Supervise the implementation of the itinerary.

★ Coordinate the relationship between tourists and the local tour guide.

★ Deal with individual requests and unexpected situations.

团队到达目的地城市后，领队/全陪须与地陪配合完成导游服务。提供服务时，须以地陪为主、领队/全陪为辅的合作模式进行。此外，领队/全陪还应做好以下工作:

☆ 行程中注意观察和收集旅游者的意见。

☆ 监督地接社执行计划。

☆ 协调旅游者和地陪的关系。

☆ 处理旅游者个别要求和突发事件。

169. How should tour guides cooperate with drivers to provide good services?（导游应如何与司机合作提供优质服务？）

★ Respect drivers. The tour guide should introduce the driver to tourists in the first presentation. After the farewell speech, suggest tourists thank the driver for his/her services.

★ Ensure effective communication. Inform the driver of the schedule in advance; before setting off, the tour guide should fully communicate with the driver about the route, parking site, meeting place etc., avoiding interfering the driver when he is driving; communicate timely if there is any change in the itinerary; when announcing the meeting time and place for inbound tourists, do not forget to tell the driver.

★ Assist drivers in ensuring safe driving. Make sure the schedule is not too tight; assist the driver in safety inspection work; avoid idle chit-chat with the driver, but during long trips, the tour guide should make an effort to talk to the driver to help keep them alert.

☆ 尊重司机。导游在首次讲解前，应当将司机介绍给旅游者。欢送词结束后，应建议旅游者感谢司机的服务。

☆ 做好沟通工作。提前将活动日程告知司机，在车辆启动之前与司机充分沟通行车路线、停靠站点、集合上车点等，避免在行车过程中影响司机正常驾驶；如有行程变化要及时沟通；入境团队在宣布集合时间地点后，也要告诉司机。

☆ 协助司机做好安全行车工作。在行车的时间安排上，留有余地；协助司机做好安全检查工作；不与司机闲聊，但长途行车时，为避免司机犯困，导游应主动与司机说话。

【备注】如接待的是入境团队，导游在建议旅游者感谢司机时，应让司机知晓。如旅游者将小费都给地陪，地陪应根据情况灵活处理。

Related words and phrases

presentation spot	讲解点
national schedule	全程接待计划
route	游览路线

consultation	咨询
convey information	传达信息
teamwork	团队合作
peak season	旅游旺季
off season	旅游淡季

Questions for discussion

1. If you are a national guide, what will you do to deal with the incident that a tourist comes to you and complains that the local guide is not kind enough to help borrow an adaptor?
2. If you are the tour leader, the tight schedule of the group in Europe results in daily longer running hours of the coach, which is in violation of EU's rule on daily driving hour limit. Thus the driver refuses to follow the schedule. What will you do?

Unit 16

听力音频

Unit 16 The Art of Managing a Tour 导游带团艺术

170. List some possible reasons that tourists might complain.（列举一些可能会引发旅游者投诉的原因。）

Tour guides usually face the following complaints:

★ When some new tour guides speak too fast, tourists may miss what they are talking. In this case they may complain of tour guides' poor language competence.

★ When the tour guide is making narration on the coach, tourists can't hear the guide talking as the microphone is of bad condition or the engine at the back of the coach is too noisy.

★ In the hotel, tourists might complain that their room is smoky or the water closet doesn't work at all. If the hotel room is not well sound-proof, tourists might complain that they can't sleep well at night.

★ When tourists are having dinner in the local restaurants, they might complain the food is not hot enough. The vegetarian might want to have more choices while the restaurants only prepare Tofu or bok-choy which is too simple. After tourists have had quite a few Chinese meals, they might complain that most meals are the same.

★ Tourists are of different ages, careers and educational background, so they have different expectations from tour guides. Some new tour guides may find it difficult to adjust themselves to different groups. If the guide can't answer questions raised by tourists or the guide ignores the tourists' special requests, tourists will complain.

★ Most foreign tourists don't like surprises. If there are uncertain situations that may affect the tour, the tour guide had better let the tourists know beforehand.

导游有可能接到以下投诉：

☆ 有些新导游讲解语速很快，旅游者没听明白导游的讲解。在这种情况下，旅游者会投诉导游的语言能力欠佳。

☆ 当导游在旅游车上讲解时，由于麦克风效果不好或是因为后排引擎的噪声太大，导致旅游者听不见讲解。

☆ 在酒店，旅游者可能会抱怨房间有烟味或者洗手间不好用。如果房间不隔音，旅游者会抱怨他们整夜无法入睡。

☆ 旅游者在餐厅用餐时，可能会抱怨菜不热。素食者希望有更多的选择但餐厅只提供简单的豆腐或白菜。旅游者吃过几顿中餐后常常会抱怨菜品没变化。

☆ 旅游者年龄、职业和教育背景各不相同，他们对导游的要求也是不同的。一些新导游很难根据不同的旅游团调整自己的服务。如果导游无法回答旅游者提出的问题，或者忽视旅游者的诉求，旅游者很容易投诉。

☆ 大多数外国人不喜欢惊喜，如果有什么可能会影响行程的不确定因素，最好提前告诉旅游者。

【备注】国外旅游者的投诉往往涉及导游的讲解、餐饮安排、住宿条件、导游综合服务素质及不确定因素导致的变化。实际操作中，对于已经解决的投诉，如不涉及违反合同原则的，导游在顺利解决后，可酌情考虑是否向旅行社汇报。如此，旅行社会认为该导游的控团能力、解决问题能力、处理事故的能力强，遇到特殊团队会优先安排。

171. How do you deal with complaints?（如何应对旅游者投诉？）

★ Be patient with tourists' complaint.

★ If the complaint makes sense, sincerely apologize for the inconvenience arising from it and promise to do something to improve your work.

★ If the complaint gives a rise to serious consequence, report it to the office and wait for the instruction to resolve it.

★ Handle complaints according to law and regulation; minimize the side effects of the case.

★ Keep a record of the case when the tour is over.

☆ 耐心听取旅游者投诉。

☆ 如旅游者投诉合理，向他们表示诚恳道歉，并承诺改进工作。

☆ 如投诉内容已造成严重后果，报告旅行社等待指示。

☆ 依法答复，依规处理，尽量降低事件负面影响。

☆ 行程结束后，提交报告留档。

【备注】面对旅游者投诉，导游首先要耐心地听取意见。"听"包括五个层次：同理心倾听、专心地听、有选择地听、假装听和忽略地听。导游在面对旅游者投诉时，首先应带着理解的愿望去听，而不是准备去回应，即同理心倾听。如果导游对每一次投诉能收集尽可能多的信息，并跟踪所收到的所有投诉，了解这些投诉是如何处理的以及处理的最佳方法。就可以用这种方式可以持续提升他/她的服务质量。(If the guide can gather as much information regarding the complaint as possible and then keep track of all the complaints he/she has received, how these complaints are dealt with and which methods appear to work the best, the guide may keep improving his/her service.)

172. What will you do when someone blames everything unpleasant on you?（当旅游者将所有不满归因于导游时，你会如何处理？）

★ If part of his/her complaint is related to your service and makes sense, sincerely apologize. Let it be known that you will try everything possible to improve your work.

★ If his/her complaints don't make any sense at all, smile and say "Let me think about it and see what I can do."
★ If his/her complaint is related to the arrangement of the program, transportation vehicles, food, etc., notify the office and try to find out whether something can be done to ease the grievance of the tourist.
★ If all your efforts are in vain to calm down the tourist who complains all the time due to his/her own emotional or psychological reasons, try to get better understanding and support from the great majority of the group.

☆ 如旅游者投诉的部分内容与导游服务有关并有一定的道理，导游应诚恳道歉并承诺尽力改进工作。
☆ 如投诉内容完全不合理，仍应保持微笑并灵活应对，如回答："让我看看，能为您做些什么？"
☆ 如投诉涉及行程安排、交通工具、餐饮等，导游应向旅行社及时反映并尽力缓解旅游者的不满情绪。
☆ 如旅游者因个人情绪或心理原因，事事抱怨，而导游的所有努力均无明显效果，那就尽量争取赢得绝大多数旅游者对自己工作的理解和支持。

【备注】导游是旅游业中与各要素关联最多的从业人员，是各种矛盾和利益关系的交会点，也因此成为目前中国旅游市场乱象频发的焦点。在诸多旅游投诉中，导游这个群体已成为民众关注甚至指责的对象。化解旅游者不满情绪、应对旅游者投诉的能力是一名合格导游必备的工作能力。

173. How will you establish a good relationship with the central figure of the group?（导游带团中该如何处理好与旅游团“中心人物”的关系？）

★ Recognize the central figure as soon as possible.

★ Respect them.

★ If there are any problems, the tour guide should ask for their advice sincerely and respectfully so as to satisfy their self-esteem and sense of honor. And in this way, the tour guide may also win their support.

☆ 导游人员要尽快识别“中心人物”。

☆ 尊重“中心人物”。

☆ 遇到问题，导游要主动找他们做工作，真诚有礼貌地与其商量，以满足他们的自尊心和荣誉感。如此，导游也可以赢得他们的支持。

【备注】本题中的“the central figure”，也可用“the influencer”，意指此类“中心人物”的态度通常会影响、引导团队其他成员。

174. How can a tour guide recognize the central figure in the group quickly?（导游如何快速辨别出旅游团的“中心人物”？）

★ In most cases, the tour guide may consult the tour leader, or the guide may recognize them by observing the group.

★ The central figures have high prestige in the group and their attitude is often followed by the rest of the group.

★ They generally have three characteristics: he/she has rich social experience; he/she is knowledgeable and strong-minded; he/she is skillful at dealing with various problems.

☆ 通常情况下，导游可以咨询领队，或者导游可以通过自己的观察来辨别。

☆ “中心人物”在团队中很有威望，他们的态度常常会影响团队其他成员。

☆ “中心人物”一般有三个特点：一是有比较丰富的社会阅历；二是认知能力比较强，且意志比较坚定；三是有比较娴熟的社会交往技巧。

175. What precautions should be taken by the tour guide to prevent tourists from getting lost?（为预防旅游者走失，导游应采取哪些防范措施？）

★ Remind tourists from time to time.

(1) Important information such as the name and phone number of the travel agency and hotel should be repeated. Ask tourists to keep the phone number of the tour guide.

(2) Tell tourists the detailed arrangement, including the name and address of the restaurant.

(3) At each spot, repeatedly inform tourists of the parking place, car number, orientation and characteristics of the parking lot, meeting time and place. Before entering the attractions, emphasize the meeting time and place.

(4) Remind tourists to follow the group.

(5) When tourists are free, tell tourists not to go to crowded or remote places and return to the hotel as soon as possible at night.

★ Count the number of the group frequently.

★ Cooperate with the tour leader and the national guide.

☆ 加强提醒，做好预报。

(1)反复向旅游者告知地接社电话和名称、酒店名称电话、导游手机号。

(2)预报当天行程，包括餐厅名称和地址。

(3)每到一个景点，反复告知停车地点、车牌号、方位、特征，强调集合开车时间。进入景点游览前，再次讲清游览时间、集合时间和集合地点。

(4)提醒旅游者随团活动。

(5)自由活动时不要去拥挤或偏僻的地方，晚间尽早回到酒店。

☆ 坚持随时清点人数。

☆ 地陪与全陪及领队分工合作，共同管理。

【备注】对于重点团队，可以制作发放"应急联系卡"，卡上有中英文的导游联系方式和地接社紧急联系方式。

176. How can you tell tourists the importance of punctuality in a smart way?（你会用何种方式告知旅游者守时的重要性？）

★ The guide may discuss with the whole group on the importance of punctuality on the first day.

★ You may tell the tourists, "I am glad to be your guide. We will visit the city as a group. Punctuality is very important for any group. So I hope all of us can be punctual. If anyone is late for more than 15 minutes, we may assume that he/she wants to visit the city alone. So we will not wait for him/her. Is that fair?"

★ In most cases, tourists may agree that those who are late for more than 15 minutes should be left behind.

☆ 导游可以在接团第一天就此问题与旅游者讨论。

☆ 可以跟旅游者这么说："很荣幸成为大家的导游。我们团队将一起游览这个城市。遵守时间对团队来说很重要。希望大家都能准时。如果有旅游者比约定集合时间晚 15 分钟以上，我们就认为他/她想独自游览这个城市，所以我们将不会继续等他/她，大家觉得这样处理合理吗？"

☆ 在大多数情况下，旅游者会同意不用等候那些迟到的旅游者。

【备注】有了事先公开的讨论，旅游者一般会尽量守时，即便因不守时而落单，旅游者也少有投诉。另外，在“守时”这个问题上，不同的文化有不同的态度。譬如，印度旅游者的时间观念与欧美很多国家旅游者的观念不同，在带团时也要具体问题具体对待。通常印度旅游者的团队约定出发时间要比实际出发时间晚10~15分钟。

177. What will you do if the questions raised by tourists are beyond you?（如果无法回答旅游者提出的问题怎么办？）

★ Honesty is best policy. Sometimes you have to admit that you know very little about the question asked by the tourists. Meanwhile, you should tell tourists that you will find the answer as soon as possible. You may say, “Thank you for the question. But frankly speaking, I know very little about it. I am sorry for that. Can I check it with some experts and tell you later?”

★ Sometimes you may handle it in a smart way. For example, you may tell the tourists, “That is a great question. But you see, time is limited, shall we discuss it later?” Then you may surf the Internet or ask some experienced tour guides for help. Don’t forget to reply to tourists.

☆ 诚实是最好的策略。有时导游应当承认自己对旅游者提出的问题知之甚少。同时，导游应当告诉旅游者，你会尽快解答这个问题。导游可以这么说：“感谢您的提问，非常抱歉对此我不是很清楚，我会尽快咨询这方面的专家并及时回复您。”

☆ 当然，导游也可以用其他方式解决这一问题。比如，可以跟旅游者说：“这个问题很棒，不过此刻时间比较紧，我们待会儿有空再讨论。”然后，赶紧上网查询或咨询有经验的导游。但要记得及时回复旅游者。

178. What will you do if tourists insist on discussing some sensitive topics?（如果旅游者抓住敏感问题紧追不放怎么办？）

★ As a tour guide, you should get yourself well prepared for some common sensitive and controversial topics.

★ It is not wise to ignore their questions. Instead, you should answer their questions carefully in order to eliminate misunderstanding.

★ In view of the question proposed by tourists, you may give an introduction to our country's situation. Tell them the position and viewpoint of our government.

★ If tourists still insist on their opinions, don't try to persuade them. Instead, you should seek common ground.

★ In face of malicious attacks, you should refute, avoiding entanglement with them.

★ For most sensitive and controversial questions, you may respond by saying, "We have different sources of information. So it is natural that we have different attitudes towards this matter. As far as I know ... *(briefly share your opinion on the topic)*. I am afraid you may have different opinions, but that is my knowledge about the topic. Let's agree to disagree."

☆ 导游对一些常见的敏感且有争议的问题，应提前做好准备。

☆ 试图忽略这些问题是不明智的；相反，应认真地回答旅游者提出的问题，以消除误解。

☆ 导游要针对旅游者提出的问题友好地介绍我国国情，阐明我国政府的立场、观点。

☆ 若见解不一致，不必强求，求同存异。

☆ 若遇恶意攻击和诬蔑，应观点鲜明地予以驳斥，但应避免与之纠缠。

☆ 对大多数敏感且有争议的问题，你可以这样回答旅游者"我们信息渠道不同，所以对这一问题我们持有不同的态度是很正常的。就我所知……（简明扼要地介绍你对问题的看法）。您可能有不同的看法，就此事，我们求同存异吧。"

【备注】热爱祖国是我国导游人员的首要条件。海外旅游者常会通过导游的言谈举止来观察、了解中国。涉外导游人员还应了解国际形势和热点问题，以及中国的外交政策和对有关国际问题的态度。这绝不是空话，工作中我们发现对外国旅游者非善意言论盲目附和的导游，往往得不到旅游者的尊重；反倒是言谈举止得体，对敏感问题正面回答的导游最受旅游者尊重。另外，对一些敏感问题要有预判，提前准备并灵活应对。如西方旅游者在上海游览完玉佛寺后，往往会询问中国的宗教政策、“西藏问题”、民族问题等。恰好上海玉佛寺边上有一所学校，笔者通常在游览玉佛寺结束后，立刻顺势讲解上海的教育情况。如此操作，基本可以避免客人就宗教、民族、西藏等话题提问。

Related words and phrases

controversial issues	有争议的问题
human rights	人权
religious problems	宗教问题
theism	有神论
atheism	无神论
Taoism	道教
Confucianism	儒教；儒家
Buddhism	佛教
Islam	伊斯兰教
Christianity	基督教
Orthodox	东正教
Protestantism	新教
Catholicism	天主教
church	教堂
mosque	清真寺

temple	寺庙
Taoist temple	道观
Ohel Moishe Synagogue	摩西会堂

Questions for discussion

1. How will you respond to a complaint that a silk quilt bought in the designated store is overcharged?
2. What will you do when some tourists want to visit some special places for better understanding of the Cultural Revolution?

NOTES

NOTES

NOTES

NOTES